CU00417448

Con

PART I

INTRODUCTION

Today is the first of May. It is mid-day. The sun shines brightly on the smooth and gently flowing Thames, as its waters sweep from Kingston to Richmond. Half-way stands the oak under which he who sang the "Hymn to the Seasons" sat gazing listlessly on the tranquil stream—emblem of his own mind. Sojourning long in a strange land he had adopted it for his own; its scenery, sky, river, people. He had exchanged the banks of the crystal Tweed for the still more placid Thames, and the peaceful highly cultivated vale of Roxburgh for a still more fertile land. They differ but little; and thus, whether on Tweed side or by Thames bank, whether at Roxburgh or Kingston, the bard from Scotland but not of Scotland, was an English poet; not so immortal Burns: your mind and your country were one. You alone portrayed in telling words the scenes of which I am about to speak. Ayr and Doone, Yarrow and Tweed, Annan and Nith, Gala and Ettrick; to the banks of these rivers and streams, and waters, let me lead the angler, and show him what true angling means. I sit by Thames bank, but "My heart is not here" neither is it in "the highlands" which is not a true angling country, but by the margin of lone and desolate Fastna, or by St. Bathan's ruined abbey, or by Chirnside Bridge, tempting with fly and minnow the spotted trout and silvery salmon. Here on Thames bank I see some one sitting in a boat, holding in his hand what resembles a fishing-rod. Do you call this angling? Yes; it is angling in England. Be it so; but it bears no resemblance to angling anywhere else. Even Izaak's angling is rather prosy, but compared with this thing in the punt, it was at least refreshing. Old Izaak! Model angler of a model nation; I should like to see one of your disciples fish the lone and desolate Fastna, with no resting-place between its eldrid bridge and Elmsford. How little does he know of angling who has merely fished the preserved streams and ponds of fat and prosperous England.

A word on angling in England. I sojourned for a year or two in the south of England, a short way from the muddy banks of the Southampton water, in Hampshire; where the vine, uncherished by artificial heat, yet yielded tolerable fruit. Some friends, fond of angling for trout, invited me to accompany them to a preserved stream of the river which, descending from Stockbridge, unites at last with the Itchen, thus forming the Southampton water.

It was a warm autumnal day. My friend drove us in his handsome chariot and pair to the scene of action. From the proprietor of the estate and of the right to fish we had a hearty welcome and proceeded at once to the banks of the stream. To me the scene was new, although a perusal of "The Complete Angler" had to a certain extent prepared me for it.

A gently flowing, quiet muddy stream, deeply fringed with sedge, and full to the brink, somewhat like a ditch about to overflow, meandered, if you will, through fat, artificially irrigated meadows. The pasture was knee deep, rank and marshy. Clumps of willows studded the landscape; here and there little wooden bridges crossing the deep irrigating canals, relieve the listlessness and monotony of the scene. On one of these there sat a reverend pastor of a class of which Paley was the type. He seemed weighty enough to be an archdeacon. A boy carried his angling apparatus and a seat for him to rest occasionally. He was in accordance with the scenery and the scenery with him.

Our party in the meantime tried boldly for trout, but were unsuccessful; nevertheless, it is certain that occasionally some fine trout are caught here, for the rivers of Hampshire are noted for the excellence, if not abundance, of their trout and salmon.

An esteemed friend, G——, of the Guards, a Saxon and an Englishman, assures me that English anglers must not be despised. They fish "under hand" that is the phrase, and take many *brace of trout*, where the overhand northern could take nothing. Very likely they know the temper of their own fish, and the character of their becks and rivers; the taste and habit of the fish of their own country. And in one respect they have the advantage greatly over most of the northern anglers; the fish they take, especially in the south of England, are as excellent as those of Scotland are generally worthless. The red-spotted river trout of England, frequenting the fresh water only, is, generally speaking, a much finer fish than the species usually met with in the Scottish rivers. The northern is a coarser fish, tasteless, colourless, or nearly so, in its muscle or flesh; the trout of the south of England is a handsomer trout, with pink-coloured flesh, and excellent to eat. This does not depend on the food, but mainly on their being specifically distinct. Nevertheless, the pink or pale salmon-coloured trout is also to be met with in many streams of Scotland; in the Tyne, the water of Leith, the Eden, as I shall afterwards show; whilst, no doubt, the coarser or Scottish kind is to be also met with in some parts of England, especially in the north. I have always heard that the trout of the Coquet are as worthless as those of the Tweed and its tributaries. But to return. A sumptuous dinner and choice wines awaited our return to the house of our host; the carriage was ordered about ten, and so we reached home without other fatigue than that of sitting three or four hours over our dinner and wine.

As I stood on the banks watching the movements of the Vicar, for such he was at the least, on the other side, and of my more active friends on this, I said to myself, this no more resembles true angling than does yonder swelling upland with its patches of heath the desolate and lonely glens of the Lammermuir; the muddy stream before me, the silver, crystal Tweed; the air I breathe, stagnating over these fat meadows, the honey-
wafting, pure, refreshing, exhilarating, life-restoring gale, which blows over Priestlaw on a summer morn."

Away, then, I said, to the lonely glens and mountain tops of the true angling country, Scotland, in fancy, at least, if not in reality. I will describe, I said, angling in Scotland, as I have experienced it.

I say this without meaning to disparage English rivers and angling in them. I see, in fact, that, under certain circumstances, some excellent trout are to be caught in rivers, such as I have described. But the angler would, I think, require to be differently equipped, and his matériel more artistically finished than is requisite on Scottish rivers and lakes. There is first the permission to be obtained; next, as to equipment, long waterproof boots, to wade and splash through the marshy meadows; the finest tackle, a small salmon-rod, with several spare tops; abundance of live minnows of all sizes, and a choice of flies. The small streams and rivulets called becks, in the north of England, and no doubt in the south, abound with good trout of at least two kinds. Cautious fishing with worm or minnows, dropped very cunningly just over the bank, is sure to succeed. I have practised this often in Scotland. But of all this I shall speak more hereafter. In the meantime, let me dismiss, as briefly as may be what kinds of trout and fish of the salmon kind are to be caught in Scotland by the angler, it being best for him to know what he is to expect; what matériel and equipment will best suit him, and how he is to proceed; and finally, conduct him to the rivers and lakes themselves, and there discuss with him many nice and difficult questions, which closet, naturalists, learned though they be, have failed to solve.

1st. Of the kinds of trout and of salmon which are caught in Scotland, and in the rivers and lakes of the Border country.

Although it be easy enough in general to distinguish at a glance a fresh-water trout from a sea trout, and both these from the true salmon, more especially when all three have attained their adult condition, yet this kind of knowledge, though highly practical and useful, being, in fact, what constitutes the skill of the experienced fishmonger, will be found far behind that which the angler requires or desires to know in respect of the beauteous finny tribe, for which he angles. The naturalist, it is true, is bound, as a naturalist, to take note only of the fully-developed adult individual; this he carefully examines and describes, recording its characteristic features in the great Book of Nature - the *systema naturae*, in fact, of his adoption, whether that system be a modified one, dressed up by himself, or a ready-made one, the production of a master-mind; a Linné, a Buffon, a Cuvier, a De Blainville. But no good observer, not even the angler, will or ought to stop here. He does not always catch the full-grown fish; many little ones and young ones are taken, differing widely from the full-grown, though of the same kind, not yet individualized, and therefore not readily recognisable; yet he would like to know what they are - what they would become. Are they trout, or salmon, or salmon-trout? and if merely trout, to what species or kind do they belong?

It is with the hope of assisting the angler, and the curious observer of Nature's works, that I here offer him the following brief sketch of some of the results of countless angling excursions, reserving for other sections of this little book a more minute account of what the angler may meet with in Scotland.

In the rivers and lakes of Scotland, in so far as I have fished them, there are three distinct natural families of salmons, forming the genera of naturalists; to each of these belong several species absolutely distinct, whatever my esteemed friend, M. Valenciennes, may say to the contrary.

Of the genera, or natural families, there is 1st, the Salmo Salar, or Trout; some call this the Fario. I recommend the angler to eschew all pedantry.

2nd. The Salmo Trutta, or Sea Trout, universally called "Trout" simply, by the salesman.

3rd. The Salmo, or true Salmon.

These three natural families have many characteristic differences, which, when present, will enable the observer always to distinguish them from each other, even although the external robe, with its various spots and colouring were either accidentally destroyed, or altered by disease, or deeply affected, as it sometimes is, by an approach on the part of the fish to its spawning or foul condition. Of these three characteristic marks I shall here mention only the teeth, placing before the reader

1st. The dentition of the trout.

2nd. The dentition of the sea trout.

3rd. The dentition of the salmo when adult, that is perfect inasmuch as any animal condition can be esteemed perfect.

Look into the mouth of the first river or lake trout you meetwith of a good size, and you will see in the upper jaw or roof of the mouth—1st, An uninterrupted row of teeth, extending around nearly the whole margin of the mouth. These teeth, being all of one kind, are characterized, not as in mammals or in man, by different names expressive of their functions (incisors, canine, molars); but by the bones supporting them, namely, maxillary and intermaxillary, palatine, etc.

2nd. Now within these, or nearer to the mesial or middleplace or line of the mouth, is a second semi-circular row of teeth, interrupted, however, at two points. These are called vomerine teeth, being carried on two bones, which anatomists generally agree to call palatal bones. In the middle line of the palatal and between these last described, you may now observe vomerine teeth, a double alternating undulating row of teeth, extending from before backwards, separated from the palatal by clear toothless spaces, the points of the teeth being turned outwards, and so arranged as if they occupied a ridge not sufficiently broad to hold them symmetrically or side by side in pairs, hence alternating. These characteristic teeth are called vomerine or vomerian. I have occasionally called them middle palatal, for they occupy the middle line of the palatal, for the bone supporting them is presumed to be the vomer, and they form the key adopted by many naturalists to the Generic distinctions of the salmonia of every description.

The figures given here represent the palate in the three natural families of the salmonidæ, namely -

The common trout adult.

The salmon trout   "

The true salmon "

But I caution the reader to remember, that this classification of the salmonidæ based on the teeth, is not sufficiently comprehensive to include all; for we shall find, that there are river trout which have transverse teeth on the fore part of the vomer, even in the adult state, and in this resembling the young sea trout and salmon; for they, when young, have a double row of vomerine teeth which they lose as they grow older.

To render all this more distinct, I have caused to be represented here, the said vomer, with the vomerine teeth, as they occur in the presumed adult, in the three natural families of Salmonia. The question as to what is the dentition of the young of these three natural families, opens up an inquiry which need not be entered on here. It will find a fitting place in some future chapter of this book, which the angler may perhaps peruse when, wearied with angling, he reposes on some sunny bank, before him the crystal stream full of trout, the stepping stones over which have tripped many light hearts now cold and pulseless; the ruined abbey telling of a race and a worship now dead and gone; the wooded bank, a vestige of that forest through which roamed the ancient inhabitants of Caledonia; shall we ascend further into the records of time? Yes. Look at that tiny fish in your hand, just escaped from below the gravel into a world of waters; observe it carefully; study it deeply; mark its forms; for they are vestiges of a former world. That little fish, some two or three inches long, so strongly resembling a common trout in its shape, its colouring, its dentition, is probably a salmon; yet it has the teeth and robe of the trout! Mysterious fact, explicable only by the great minds of the earth, by Newton, Goethe, Geoffroy! It was you who first proclaimed unity of the organization of all that lives. The salmon kind form no exception to this great law; when tiny and young they all resemble each other, assuming with time the specific characters which mark their adult condition. Thus does the young salmon gradually lay aside that elongated fin which connects his formation with worlds past and gone; next, the red spots and cross-bars allying him with the river trout of both kinds; by and by a robe of silvery scales conceals all vestiges of his early years; and last, not least, the double row of teeth which carried on the body of the vomer all but disappear, leaving merely one or two, together with those on the fore part of the vomer (the chevron), which few full-grown fresh-water trout when grown, admitting their presence when young, retain.

But whether or not you may choose thus to wander back in time, endeavouring to discover the unknown in the Past, and to find its demonstration in the Present, you will not, I trust, imitate old Izaak, who, living in London, and fishing all the rivers about that centre, could coolly record in his Complete Angler that "the Fordich trout" a good trout too, "was never known to rise at an angle" and yet make not one journey to discover what might be the reason of this! Happy, contented Izaak! you were never troubled with the desire to discover the unknown in the past nor in the present; sufficient for you was the fact that it is so. You were a linendraper, it is true; but Franklin was a printer, a working man. Nevertheless, it is pleasant to see what a refreshing book may be written by one devoid of genius to observe anything, but simply blessed with a love of nature sufficiently strong to narrate what he felt and saw. Izaak wrote two hundred years ago.

To return to the dentition of trout and salmon. Whilst the three families of salmons have in the upper jaw maxillary, intermaxillary, palatine and vomerine teeth, and in the lower jaw mandibular (those in the tongue being called lingual, and these also are present in all the families), yet the vomerine are differently arranged in each. For the common trout the vomerine teeth are arranged in a double alternating row, and they hold their ground even in the largest, but are generally confined to what anatomists call the body of the vomer, that is, the elongated back part of the bone. To this, however, as I have already remarked, some species offer an exception. For the grown sea trout, however (the salmo Trutta), the vomerine teeth are arranged in a single row on the body of the bone, whilst a transverse row occupies the forepart of the vomer, which French naturalists call chevron. For the true salmon, on the other hand, when fully grown, the double alternating row of teeth formed on the body of the vomer when it was a smolt, and the single row which remained for a time after the double row had disappeared, are now themselves reduced to one or two on the forepart of the body of the bone, the transverse teeth on those of the chevron remaining to the last.

Thus you may, by putting your finger into the mouth of the fish, tell, without looking at it, whatever be its size, to which of these natural families it belongs; but this does not apply to the young of these families, for the same dentition prevails in all.

Now, if every individual of the great family of the salmonidæ, including all trout and salmon, could be brought within this law, then, for the first time, I believe, since science began to be cultivated, the natural history system invented by man would be in accordance with Nature's system or plan; and the great formalist, the puffed up systematic" would swell and strut and point to his achievement, how he had discovered Nature's plan, arranged her works and omitted nothing. But unfortunately for him, and his schemes and methods and formulae, Nature never does her work in this way, but fills up all intervals, leaving no void space in her grand scheme. In the course of the present work I shall mention a fish which externally resembles a salmon, but in its vomerine teeth combines the dentition of the trout and sea trout; and, no doubt, there exist species of the great class Salmonidæ, which not only fill up the voids in the natural families, and in all the species, but even connect these with other fishes, on which the name Salmonidæ would be improperly bestowed.

Now, in regard to the species of the three great natural families have already named, I may observe, that in Scotland there are at the least, four distinct species of trout, namely:

1st. The dark-spotted lake trout.

2nd. The red-spotted estuary trout.

These are the best of their kind, they have pink-coloured flesh, and are excellent to eat.

3rd. The red-spotted common river trout, with pale flesh, and tasteless.

4th. The pink-coloured red-spotted common river trout, chiefly found in England.

5th. The parr trout, rather better, when fed in certain rivers, than the common red-spotted trout, but never equal to the pink-coloured fish.

6th. The dark-spotted river trout, of whose natural history I know but little, although I believe such a trout exists; and 7th. The Salmo Ferox, or great lake trout of the North.

II. Of the Salmo Salar, or sea trout, the angler will meet with several species, hitherto not well determined. One ascends the rivers earlier than the other; it is the common Sea Trout. The other takes to the freshwater streams at a later period of the year; it is the so-called Bull Trout.

III. Of true salmon there are no doubt several species; but I have not been able to discover their characteristic differences. Lastly, of doubtful fish there is,

1st. The Parr.

2nd. A fish with the external appearance of a salmon, but with a dentition combining that of the common river trout and sea trout or salmon.

3rd. A fish strongly resembling a salmon, and almost as good to eat, which appears in the London markets early in October; it is marked all over with darkish spots, like some trout. The fish, 1 have been told, comes from Scotland, but I have not met with it there.

Enough has been said systematically about trout and salmon. I shall therefore reserve the proofs of the correctness of these opinions for the chapters in which I examine each river, brook, and lake, placing the angler by the banks, opposite some favourite and killing stream; his basket full of fish, he may, if he so choose, compare this book with Nature.

The material and equipment of an angler are not matters of indifference. Should he reside near the banks of trouting streams, the angler gradually degenerates into a mere pot-angler; he is fishing unconsciously for the kettle; neither is he very particular as to the time when, with salmon roe, or otter, or with worm, he chances to kill some stone weight of trout, emptying the stream for a period, rendering it worthless for the season, and interfering sadly with the one to come. In '51 he draws, á la Napoléon, the conscripts of '53, forestalling Nature's supplies. Such a person is no true angler; he does not rush from the smoky town, where, long pent up, debarred from fresh air, exercise, and the contemplation of Nature's work, he has become an idler and a trifler. I write not for him, neither should he have a cottage of mine near a trouting stream at any price. I write for him who, dwelling in towns, amidst what, in courtesy, I presume, to man's taste, is called a civilized humanity, becomes at last weary of the commonplace of everyday life: for him whom the carpeted room, the morning paper, the ample library, the well-supplied table, the pleasant social converse of educated friends have ceased to please: for him who instinctively feels that, ceasing to be a man as Nature made him, he is becoming a citizen—a cit! Abhorred word! I would rather dwell, as I once did, amidst the wild and now desolate dells of the Anatolo, leading at the base of the beauteous Boschberg the life of the wandering Caffre, than listlessly pace London's idly busy streets, with nothing to look at but miles of hideous brick walls, with holes in them called doors and windows. Odious commonplace! you mask humanity and mar the better part of human nature.

I shall suppose the angler about to proceed to some angling station, there to commence his operations of at least a few days

Scots, wham Bruce has often led,
On to glorious victory!"

Scotland, by her own act, has been blotted out of the list of nations. The loss of national independence is a melancholy subject for reflection, and so 1 turn from it and from the Ammond water to other scenes and other streams.

High on the north-western slope of the Pentland, the angler will find at the distance of a morning's walk from the capital, a small stream making its way through heath and dark knolls, onwards towards the ocean. It is one of the sources of a charming stream, whose banks present the most varied and beauteous scenery; it is a tiny stream where I speak of it, that is, high on the shoulders of the Pentland range. This source of the water of Leith (for it is not the only one), crosses an uneven plain on which there are no bushes nor trees to interrupt the sport of the angler. On reaching the table-land he must not lose time. Let him select, if he can, a hot and close day, following a rainy night, summer showery-looking clouds, and having plenty of good small worms well cleaned and prepared, he may take in a short time an excellent dish of trout. When I first fished this stream in the company of the best of anglers, I was a very young angler. My friend pointed out to me the ground, recommending me to keep well back and to lose no time. In a few minutes three admirable trout lay on the bank, when suddenly all sport ceased. I could not comprehend what had happened. My friend now returned from the upper part of the stream which he had selected for his ground, and told me I might put up my rod and prepare for the road; pointing, at the same time, to a dark and lowering cloud of an inky hue collecting over Pentland's summit. It was a thundercloud—over it came, wind, rain, lightning, thunder. Then I remembered Scott's "Lady of the Lake," which was just published. Pity it ever was.

"The springing trout lies still:
So darkly lowers yon thunder cloud,

Which swathes as with a purple shroud

Benledi's distant hill."

Often, subsequently, have I observed this singular phenomenon, the explanation of which is as obscure as all other physiological laws. Why should fish - trout, at least - dread thunder? The more strange that it is in certain fishes we find that wonderful electrical apparatus connecting in so remarkable a way the laws of the electric fluid with those which regulate the nerves and brain of man.

Now why should fishes, and more especially trout, be such natural electrometers? They are called cold-blooded animals, and some have thought them insensible to pain. All this is, I fear, sheer nonsense and twaddle. But be it so, it does not explain why trout should be extremely sensible natural electrometers. It is amongst the same class, fishes, that we find natural electrometers, voltaic piles, galvanic troughs! The gymnotus of Surinam, and the torpedo of the Cape, and one or two more, strike their prey dead by an electric discharge. To accomplish this, Nature has furnished them with a peculiar apparatus she has denied to other animals, but the materials called organic are still the same, it is merely by the arrangement of a few materials that Nature accomplishes so much.

The existence of electric fishes was known to the ancients, as we call the Romans and the Greeks. Pliny, who collected so much curious nonsense, so many false facts, so many hypotheses which he mistook [for facts, knew this fact: viz. that electric fishes exist, and he records it. He knew, also, that people employed the torpedo in the treatment of rheumatism and paralysis; but whilst men are always apt enough to find out some utilitarian application of natural phenomena, no one thought of inquiring into the cause of the phenomenon. Verily, I have but a poor opinion of applicative genius—the only kind of genius possessed, it is said, by the Saxon race. It invents nothing, it merely applies. If such had been the character of the genius of Galileo, Torricelli, Volta, Newton, and Hunter, we should have been now mere recorders of facts and falsehoods, and of their "ingenious applications". That some fishes have electric powers was not enough for Hunter: he desired to know the cause thereof, and he left us his "Inquiry into the Electric Organs of the Surinam Eel" a model for all inquirers, though unfortunately it led to no physiological results. Industry, ever on the look-out to turn the penny, is no doubt a good thing. It lays the foundation for national, and occasionally for individual, wealth. By it, nations rise in the scale of civilization—indirectly, it is true, but still they rise, slowly, surely. But industry requires no stimulus, no incentive, no such prizes and laudation, as the "model nation" seems to think, at present. All men are quick enough to turn the inventions of others to account: all Saxon men, I mean—for the Celt is hopeless. Yet he also is industrious, in his own way, in the acquisition of wealth: he aims at acquiring it by the sword. England and Holland boast of their wealth acquired by patient industry; I partly doubt it. India and the Indies were not acquired by patient industry. But to return to the Esk.

Industry is a great thing, a material fact, but genius is greater. In what time Greece, by her patient industry, would have sculptured the Venus and Apollo, composed Euclid, the "Iliad", the "History of Animals," and conquered the then known civilized world, without the advent of Praxiteles, of Homer, of Euclid, Aristotle, and Alexander, I know not. But sure 1 am that the advent of these men must have assisted somewhat the "patient industry" of Greece.

Ye model people, who "cannot make a statue" let Industry alone; she requires no encouragement. Your sham patrons, of noble and ignoble blood, know this well, but it suits their purpose to mislead you, praising your foible as if it were your forte. Industry! labour! order! Excellent claptraps, which admit of a translation into taxation, slavery, discipline.

After rains, in soft, warm summer weather, trout, and most excellent ones too, may be taken as readily in the water of Leith as in any other stream, notwithstanding the abundance of mills which intercept its course. The village of Currie, about six miles from Edinburgh, used to be a good station, and even much lower. The excellent and kind-hearted angler to whom I have alluded, used to fish the river at the dam-head of Colt's bridge, scarcely two miles from Edinburgh. But on these occasions he fished at night, with the finest tackle and with the smallest midge-flies, dressed on a single hair or gut. With these he caught large trout, weighing occasionally two pounds, and of the finest flavour, for the water of Leith possesses the kind of trout found chiefly in the south of England, and but rarely in Scotland, "the red-spotted pink-coloured trout of rivers frequenting streams above the influence of the tide"

I never met with any par in the Leith, owing, probably, to there being no salmon; but I will not avouch this to be the sole cause, for I shall speak by and by of rivers in which salmon, or, at least, sea trout, abound, which yet are without par. But of this more hereafter.

On a warm autumnal morning, fresh and pleasant, heavy rains having fallen the day before, my companion and I took the road to Glencorse; but before reaching that we thought it were wise to strike the stream called Glencorse Burn, at Auchindinny bridge, a lovely and sequestered spot, within a two hours' walk of Edinburgh. As we neared the bridge, an angler appeared on the opposite bank: the honest angler is always civil and often liberal, so we hailed him. In a few minutes we three were seated on the southern bank, a short way below the bridge, and the contents of his basket turned out on the greensward for our inspection. He told us his adventure. Starting long before daybreak from Dalkeith - pleasant Dalkeith! - near Musselburgh, he reached the stream above Glencorse, fishing it from that point downwards to where we met him. His rod and flies were free to our inspection, as were the two-and-a-half dozen pretty good trout he had caught that morning. His flies were the moderate size red hackle; his lines without pretension: he was no experienced angler, but knowing enough to fish the waters after floods, when trout will bite at anything and fear nothing.

He had caught no large trout, which would not have happened had he used minnow as a bait; but he had no apparatus, and probably but little knowledge of the more refined and skilful angling for the overgrown inhabitants of the stream. He was a working man, a mechanic, living and working in a village; one of those who live in a round of ideas, a circle. In a thousand years they scarcely advance a step, and if they do, it is lost in the next ten centuries. Some think that the recession is somewhat less than the precession, and thus a something is gained in every century. Be it so; but all admit that human progress is inconceivably little—all thinking men, I mean; the great mass believes otherwise but I need not say here what I think of them. I am writing for thinking men, for anglers.

Our new acquaintance-left us, proceeding on his way; we followed shortly after. But soon heavy black clouds began to obscure the high Pentlands; rain followed as a matter of course, and by the time we had fished the burn from Auchindinny bridge to the beautiful Esk, which it joins about a mile from the bridge, it rained so heavily, that not even the shady banks of the river could protect us. We were close to the entrance of a mill, rare in the Esk; near this the trout rose at the flies two and three at a time; we took them every instant; large trout began to show themselves; they bit as freely as the smaller ones; but now it rained in torrents, and fairly drove us from the river, whilst to the last, the faster and heavier it rained the faster the trout rose at our artificial flies.

The sight of trout cannot be very good. In stormy weather ruffing the waters strongly, and in heavy rain, you may stand by the river side and take as many trout as you like, in still reaches, where there are neither rocks nor perceptible streams. The same happens in cloudy, stormy, windy weather, when the waters are clear. Along the base of Mountjoy, on the Whitwater, there is a long still reach, as straight as a canal, which, unless the waters be dark and flooded, no angler would think of fishing; for, as in walking along the banks he can see the trout, it is natural to suppose that they also see him;

nevertheless, in heavy winds, though weather and river be clear, I have fished this reach with much success, taking many good-sized trout. In the rocky streams above lie many fine trout twenty-two inches in length. But I must return to the Esk.

It was now dusk, and we sought shelter and refreshment. A small roadside thatched cottage furnished both. Next morning by break of day we were on our road to the Tweed.

At the time of which I now speak, the lovely vale of Glencorse is as Nature made it; solitary, wild, but not desolate. Now, a reservoir with its enormous embankment, intended to assist in the supply of water to the capital (in which, however, it signally failed) sadly disfigures it. The trout confined to this reservoir could no longer pass down, or at all events, none could ever again pass upwards towards the source from which the stream of Glencorse takes its rise. I have fished in this reservoir, but with no success. It has been said, that some sea trout which happened to be at the sources of the stream when the reservoir was closed, being thus cut off from their descent to the ocean, became accustomed to this artificial lake, lived, throve, and reproduced their kind. I do not believe a word of all this. The same statement had been made many years ago by a most scientific man (the late Dr. Maculloch), of a lake in the Isle of Lismore. I fear that he took the statement on hearsay. Near Guisborough, in the North Riding of Yorkshire, there is a small stream or burn, which drains the valley of Guisborough. Sea trout enter this from the sea in considerable numbers, and they breed in the rivulet. In due time, in April, or the beginning of May, the gamekeeper takes with a net a good many dozen of the fry, silvery and shining like salmon, transferring them alive to a large collection of fresh water; or artificial lake, as it were. In this, the fry, so transported, live very well for a year or two; but, from that time fall off, becoming long, lanky, black, diseased, and wholly unfit for food. Now, my information is not from hearsay, for I was present on one occasion at the. transfer of the fry to the pond. Why one result should happen in Yorkshire and another so different in the reservoir of Glencorse, I leave to be reconciled by those who say that they have caught sea trout in that reservoir, which I never did.

Man's handiwork in this lone valley has spoiled a natural glen of great beauty, desecrating ground almost classical. For here Allan Ramsay laid the scene of the "Gentle Shepherd." Allan Ramsay, of whom the noble Burns sang and wrote—

> "The tooth of time may gnaw Tantallan, But
> thou'rt for ever. "

Many years afterwards I fished the stream below the reservoir on a hot summer day; there still were trout to be taken. What surprised me was their want of strength whilst on the line. Did this arise from their being cut off from their native sources? Who can say? Man creates nothing, he simply destroys. Man is a great destroyer, but not the sole. Other unseen agencies are at work, sweeping the earth of its living inhabitants. Sauntering homewards one evening by the southern slope of the Pentland, these were my reflections.

> "Soft falls the eve on Woodhouselee"

The wooded banks of the Esk sweep far away to the east; but I look towards Woodhouselee notwithstanding, strangely enough connecting its wooded ravine with Marie Stuart. Craig Millar is in the distance, and Abercorn. The scenery will repay the angler his walk, even should his day's angling have proved unsuccessful.

Of the Esk itself, as an angling stream, I can say but little. It is too wooded. But this I believe, from what I saw at the junction of the Glencorse stream with the Esk, that in close autumnal weather, and during rains, a bold angler, with a strong rod, short line, good tackle, flies and minnows, might in the Esk, at various points, find excellent sport. But he must not regard the getting thoroughly wet, crossing the streams up to the waist. Let him beware of the deep gullies, longitudinal and precipitous, worn in the sandstone bed of the river, brim full of water, and most treacherous. A false step here might lead to destruction. Thus cautioned, I recommend the angler to traverse, as he can at various times, the beauteous banks of the Esk, from Woodhouselee to Roslin, from Roslin to the sea, if he can obtain permission. In my younger days large sea trout ascended as high as Dalkeith, pleasant Dalkeith honoured in some of Delta's sweet verse and charming prose. He will meet with scenery not to be surpassed, if equalled, of its kind, as Roslin and Hawthorndean. But the Esk is not a river to be fished by young and inexperienced anglers; no more is the Tyne, angling in which will form the subject of my next chapter.

At the mouth of the Esk is, or used to be, a stake-net, in which are taken, during the autumn especially, salmon, sea trout, and hirling. The fishermen also occasionally haul the seine from the shore, around the mouth of the old harbour, taking small sea trout and hirling. Of these I remarked this curious circum. stance: some had been feeding on the food preferred by the true salmon, and which he can only get in the sea, namely, the eggs of the Echinodermata, marine animals, called star-fish, sea-urchins, etc; but others had been feeding plentifully on sand-eels. In the former the flesh was highly coloured, like salmon; the stomach and intestines clean, semi-transparent, and all but empty: in the latter the flesh was paler, and the stomach and intestines loaded with semi-putrescent debris.

I have since made the same observation with respect to hirling and sea trout taken in the Solway; that is, that whenever they have been living on the eggs of the Echinodermata, the flesh was deep-coloured, and their stomach and intestines all but empty; the opposite being the case when sand-eels and fry formed their food. Thus food has a certain influence over the quality of fish. The rich colour of the salmon, and the excellent qualities of the flesh of the char, of the winter and spring trout of Loch Leven, do not depend altogether upon the peculiar food which it is now known these fishes prefer; but unquestionably this food is necessary to bring them to that perfection in colour and flavour which renders them so excellent. On the quality of the food then, combined with other circumstances, will depend the excellence of the fish; that is, whether or not the individual is to reach that perfection which we know to be attainable under favourable circumstances. But to this must be added specific character" and the appropriate season, without which no food can ever avail.

The flesh or muscle of the smolt (young salmon) is pale, and not much better than a common trout of the same size. It bears the same relation to the flesh of the grown fish, the adult salmon, that veal does to prime beef. Its food, it is true, is the food of the common river trout, on which, whilst in the freshwater streams, it feeds voraciously. But descending to the sea, it in a very few months, nay, even weeks, rapidly attains maturity. What in the meantime has happened? 1st, it has grown, and become matured; 2nd, it has obtained in great abundance, no doubt, the real food its instincts prompt it to feed on; 3rd, it breathes a marine air, as nature intended it should.

The streams, then, which run from the Pentland range contain the red-spotted pink-coloured trout, analogous, if not identical, with that of England. The common red-spotted trout, coarse and tasteless, is also there; yet I mention it as somewhat remarkable that, in as far as my experience goes, admirable trout, not inferior to those of England, are sometimes caught in the artificial ponds of Abercorn; ponds fed by a rivulet called Clear Burn, a short way from Edinburgh. Indeed, it is not improbable that most of the trout taken in these streams, if allowed to grow to a proper age, would prove of the pink-coloured kind, and excellent as food. But they are generally caught when small; their flesh then has neither the colour nor flavour of the full-grown trout; this they can only acquire with time.

I regret that I cannot put my hands on any notes respecting the natural history of the red-spotted pink-coloured river trout of Scotland; and cannot therefore say whether or not they are identical with those of England. In lieu thereof, I may offer the angler, in a future chapter, some observations on the trout of England, which I consider as analogous, if not identical, with the trout caught in the stream I am about to describe; for it is in the Tyne, of which I have next to speak, that trout are found which would not discredit the Itchen or the Thames.

I subjoin a few notes respecting the salmonidæ taken with nets at the mouth of the Esk (near Musselburgh), one of the many small streams which pour their waters into the Firth of Forth.

Notes respecting the food of the sea trout and hirling, taken at the mouth of the Esk, Firth of Forth.

Stake-net fishings at Fisherow. - The runners were not found essential; the tenant also fished the shores with a coble and very fine meshed net, able to take anything, and similar to what we saw used on the Nith. With this he took some sea trout of six pounds weight, and many fish which he called hirlings: to me they looked exactly like the hirlings of the Nith and Solway. Eight were examined, each about fourteen inches long, male and female nearly equal; neither ova nor milt were developed, flesh not so good as in those of the Annan, ascribed by me at the time to their food, for in all, the stomachs were loaded with the fry of herrings and sand-eels in all stages of solution, the red substance (ascertained to be the eggs of the Echinodermata)t being wanting. This kind of food was almost constantly found in the stomachs of the hirlings of the Nith and Solway. On the 4th of September of the same year, seven more whilings or hirlings were examined at Fisherow; one, fifteen inches long. This was excellent eating; it contained in its stomach and intestines the reddish substance, but nothing else (eggs of the Echinodermata) in the stomach and intestines. The other six were like the previous one, both as to their food and condition when used as food.

CHAPTER II

THE TYNE

I have ever preferred angling in summer and in autumn, though well aware that April and May fishings are excellent. The trouts are ready, and have got, or are getting, into good order; but the land is not, and the forests are black and leafless. In April and in May the ground is drear, and cold, and black in Scotland, and even in England. I prefer, therefore, June or July, August and September, and even October, though late for sport. I love to wander by the banks of streams, and on the by-paths in lonely glens, when west winds are beginning to strew the woodlands with yellow leaves; when salmon and grilse begin to run for the mountain streams, leaving their undiscovered oceanic haunts; pensive to mark, unpinched by eastern gales and splashing rain and sleet, the water-ouzel flitting from pool to pool, the campagnole plunging beneath the overhanging bank; to listen to the turtle-dove cooing in the wooded slopes; to mark the melancholy and solitary heron standing motionless by the willow-shaded pool. In a word, let not the angler seek the Scottish rivers too early.

Springtime is beautiful, most beautiful; but there is, properly, no spring in Scotland. Until June, the country is desolate; then comes forth joyous Nature, young, fresh, reanimating the lifeless earth. But pensive autumn has also its beauties; though summer, bright and glowing, is the noontide of life.

> Let others love the city,
>   And gaudy show at sunny noon:
> Give me the lonely valley,
>   The dewy eve, and rising moon;
> Fair beaming and streaming
>   Her silver light; the boughs among.

The Tyne cannot be fished -in a day; but it may in two or three. Should the weather be favourable, the angler may still even now have good sport. Sweet spots he will pass through; lowland fields and woods, - he traverses, in fact, the valley of the Tyne, one of the richest in Scotland. I recommend him to make for Blackshiels, by coach or on foot. He will find a pleasant inn here, where he should rest for the evening, and, after an early breakfast, make for Hunbie Woods and Manse. The mill dam, though small, contains abundance of trout, but the stream lower down traverses woods which forbid all angling. He must seek for some more open ground towards Salton, where some parts of the river are still open to the angler.

In Hunbie Woods stood, a few years ago, a grand tree, supposed to have belonged to the original Sylva Caledonia of the Romans.

The Tyne drains the northern slopes of the Lammermuir from beyond Soutra to the Red Brae of Danskine. A pretty strong branch joins the Tyne running from the Red Hill of Danskine and Lammer Law, by Gifford. I never fished it, but it no doubt contains trout, for I have ate of those which were caught by boys in the neighbourhood of Danskine Inn. They were no way remarkable for their quality, any more than were those caught at Humbie; and this seems to me the more remarkable, as in the lower waters of the Tyne, from Haddington to the sea, excellent red-spotted pink-coloured trout are caught; and of the fishings from Haddington to the sea I shall now write.

The angler, in fishing the Tyne from Haddington to the sea, will be interrupted by several preserved grounds; but there is sufficient open space below them, above as well as below Hailes Castle. In these waters, fished with care, he cannot fail to take excellent trout with artificial fly and minnow. In May I have caught salmon fry close to Hailes Castle, but I never saw any parr taken in the Tyne, at any point. There lives on Tyne banks a school-fellow of my own, now I believe an earl, who, I am sure, would decide this question for me were I to write to him; and this remark I happened to make whilst enjoying the hospitality of a nobleman as fond of trout and salmon as I am myself. Now it happened that a gentleman who sat beside me at the table was a relation by marriage of my noble schoolfellow, and he therefore said that not being quite so busy as I was, he would proceed next morning to the Tyne, and decide this negative point. I heard afterwards that it was decided against me, and that par are to be found in the Tyne. They must be very few. I have angled the Tyne often at various points, and never saw one; nor met with an experienced anᵍer who had. I had baskets full of trout sent me at various times from East Linton, on the Tyne, caught for me by a most experienced angler, Mr. Ballantyne, but I never saw any parr amongst these. But be this as it may, the Tyne near Hailes Castle affords excellent fishing, and many of the trout, though red-spotted, are excellent eating, having pale rose-coloured flesh.

As we descend the Tyne to Linton, the portion of the river influenced by the tide is reached: and this point would afford good sport to the angler, were it not almost daily fished by means of a very powerful net which takes everything. Sea trout are frequently caught, and salmon occasionally, but of this I am not quite certain. But that of which I am certain is, that there are taken here, though not very abundantly, a red-spotted trout, with pale rose-coloured flesh, like sea trout, and excellent for the table. I have called it the Estuary trout, and it is specifically distinct from all others. At the end of the chapter I have briefly sketched its natural history. Its food I have ever found to be the small shrimp, which float in cone-shaped clusters, with the apex towards the back, and against the stream. My friend George Hunter, of Tynefield, an excellent angler, now fishing for gold in Australia, assured me that occasionally a trout such as I describe, might be taken with a small' artificial fly and single hair line, in the river a little lower down and close to the mouth from off the artificial bank at Tynefield. It is not improbable, but still I know that the food of this trout is peculiar, and in the great number I have examined to decide this point in their natural history nothing was ever found in their stomachs but the shrimp I have mentioned.

This "trout of the estuary," I afterwards found in the Nith similarly located, i.e., in " the waters into which the tide ebbs and flows;" waters which clearly to define has defied the legal knowledge of the three kingdoms; nay, baffled science itself, for no scientific man has yet been able to define the mouth of a river, which pours its waters directly into the sea.

I have been assured that occasionally a dark-spotted trout, of excellent flavour, and strongly resembling the Leven trout, is caught in the lower waters of the Tyne, below the falls and dam of Linton; and it has been conjectured, with some show of probability, that these trout may have left Prestmannan Lake, and found their way by the sea into the mouth of the Tyne. The theory is ingenious enough, but objections might be raised to it. Prestmannan Lake is a small artificial pool of fresh water, into which the late Mr. Robert Fergusson, of Raith, transferred many dozens of the trout from Loch Leven. Of this interesting experiment, I shall speak in the chapter on Loch Leven.

Tyne Mouth is wild and lonely; a vast sandy bay, abounding in quicksands, extends for several miles. By this the traveller, at low tide, may reach Dunbar; but it behoves him to be cautious, and not linger on the sands, nor attempt them alone. They abound in quicksands, in which man and horse have been engulfed. Over these sands the sea rolls fearfully in north-easterly gales, and on them, I think, was cast away, during the last century, the Fox man of war. Beyond these is Dunbar, no angling station, but worth a visit, were it only to look at Down Hill, where Cromwell's Ironsides cut to pieces the flower of the Scottish army; where the Mucklewraths did for their friends what they afterwards repeated at Bothwell Bridge. In fanaticism the two hosts were probably equal; they differed only in discipline. Providence favoured the disciplinarian.

THE NATURAL HISTORY OF THE TROUT OF THE ESTUARY.
SALMO ESTUARIUS.

The Estuary trout is a red-spotted, handsomely shaped trout, living in brackish waters, that is, in the mouths of tidal rivers. Its dentition resembles other trouts, but it differs specifically from the common red-spotted trout of fresh waters or rivers. The flesh is of a fine pink, or salmon-colour, and it eats as well as the best Loch Leven trout. I found the same trout in the mouth of the Nith, in a precisely similar locality, i. e., io the waters into which the tide ebbs and flows; and living on the same sort of food, that is, small shrimps, shrimps which hang in clusters by the banks. In weight it runs to four pounds or more; all that I have examined were taken with the net.

I had an opportunity of examining two trout taken with the trawl in the sea, amongst the western isles, and not far from Bute. They resembled the Estuary trout in all particulars.

In the three great systems of organs which characterize the structure, and consequently habits, of the salmonidæ, as compared with each other, namely, the respiratory and digestive (head and gills), and the locomotive, or fins, the Estuary trout holds a middle place between the Loch Leven and the common river trout; stronger than the first, abut weaker than the last. They probably belong to a large natural family of the salmonidæ, not yet investigated, at the head of which stands the many-spotted salmon, which appear in the London markets towards the end of September and beginning of October, and which, by most London fishmongers, are simply called trout. Their natural history is still to write.

I have already mentioned the curious fact that trout, quite similar if not identical with the Estuary trout, have been taken in the trawl-net in the sea and sea lochs of the Western Isles. They can live, then, in the sea. The food they prefer, and the only kind of food I have ever found in their stomachs, is a small shrimp (not at all microscopic), which abounds in estuaries and mouths of tidal rivers. The remains of these shrimps are also found in the intestines. The head of fishes, in consequence of the form and position of the gills and their gill covers, include those organs which indicate the strength of the digestive organs, and of the respiratory; that is, the jaws and the gills. Thus the size of the head, ceteris paribus, affords valuable natural history indications in respect of the habits of the species. If, in addition to these, we add the locomotive organs found in fishes, i.e. the fins and tail, we have three valuable indications of habits and points of comparison with others; specific characters, in fact, which time nor place can alter during the existing order of things, unless the extreme theories of the good Lamarck be admitted as true.

Ifr.ve now examine the trout of the estuary with reference, not so much to those spots and external colouring (though these also in a natural history sense are valuable and important), but to those grand features more immediately connected with the vital functions, comparing them with other species of the trout kind, we shall find, that the head (gills included) and fins are smaller than those of the common red-spotted trout of rivers or of the fresh waters, implying that the fish is less voracious, less active; that in its flesh it is pink-coloured and most excellent in flavour, dependent no doubt, in part, on the gammari shrimp or small shrimp on which it lives, but mainly, no doubt, on the nature of the fish itself; that the gape of the mouth is smaller than that of the common river trout, but larger than that of the Loch Leven, a fish of still more tranquil habits. Trout resembling these have been taken, as I have been assured, in the Forth, and in the Esk, in Eskdale, Yorkshire.

In August, in some of these trout, the milt was largely developed. Its teeth are nearly as large again as in the Leven trout. The pancreatic coeca are thirty-six, and the longest of these measured one inch. The dentition was as follows:

Maxillary	25	=	50
Intermaxillary	10	=	20
Palatine	14	=	28
Vomerine	10	=	20

The vertebræ are 60; floating ribs on either side 32 == 64. The peculiar parasitical insect which the salmon brings with him from the sea, is found on these trout.

I have already mentioned that this trout is not afraid of repairing to salt waters; a friend of mine saw two taken at sea off the Kyle of Bute; these I examined; and Mr. Murray, of Henderland, informed me that, off Strachur, in Loch Fine, a trout, corresponding with the one I am now describing, was caught in a net. The teeth in all amount to a hundred and fifty. Let this suffice here for the natural history of a trout which the angler may meet, with, and perhaps even take with an angle, although I never did. But although he may not be induced to angle for it, it seems right that the angler should know something about the finny tribe, and especially about so fine a trout as the one I have just described. Knowledge is a useful thing, even although it be not power. For want of a little natural history knowledge, I have seen some ludicrous mistakes made, by no means pleasant for those who made them. A young friend, a navy surgeon, told me, that being at sea, the men caught a shark whose stomach was full of the bills or mandibles of parrots and cockatoos! I showed him the mandibles of the cuttle-fish. He was confounded; he had never examined the cuttle-fish, and was not aware of the strong resemblance existing between the bills of the parrot and the beak of the cuttle-fish. Again, on seeing vast herds of antelopes grazing on the wide extended plains of Southern Africa, a poor fellow of an assistant surgeon had the misfortune to ask a brother officer if these animals preyed on each other! His character, even as a medical man, fell to zero. Lastly, Mr. T., a clever man, a lieutenant in a crack regiment of infantry, and who ought to have been a captain, for he the second to reach the top of the wall at the siege of St. Sebastian, shot a bird which the soldiers called a bustard. They had confounded bustard with buzzard, and the filthy brute he had shot (in reality a vulture) gave to him and his horse so bad an odour, as he rode with it into the camp on the banks of the Great Fish River, that for many hours they were both put in quarantine. Knowledge is a good thing, especially when practical.

A FEW DAYS' FISHING ON THE TYNE.

I select from my memoranda the results of a day's fishing on the Tyne; one of many passed on the banks of that pleasant stream.

The day was the 4th of September, warm, sunny, and beautiful; but the river was low, and boded no great sport. Yet the trout rose in great abundance notwithstanding. We commenced at Hailes Castle, and by 1pm had reached East Linton, having taken one dozen-and-a-half trout. In the afternoon, having obtained permission, we fished from the bridge at Tinningham until opposite Lord Haddington's house. The tide had begun to flow, and, in addition to some small common trout, I had the pleasure of taking with common trout fly, of rather a small size.

One female sea trout (Hirling), $9\frac{8}{8}$ by $4\frac{5}{8} = 4\frac{1}{4}$ oz.; although in wonderful condition it was decidedly weaker on the line than a trout of a similar size. It was lively only for a few seconds, and resembled in every respect (with regard to the catching) the nature of the smolt. I have preserved the skin, and shall now endeavour to describe it. Teeth numerous on the vomer, &c., very sharp pupil, smaller than that of a trout seven inches long, the roe as little altered as in the smolt, pancreatic coca very small, more so than in a trout of a similar size, everything in fact indicating the extreme youth of the animal. The stomach contained a shrimp or two and some flies, with a few other insects, but not the salmon food, although the fish must have come from the sea, not only from its appearance, but that this part of the river had been ransacked in. the morning, and every living thing taken out in preparation for Lord Haddington's arrival from London. The dorsal fin has twelve rays (nine of which are branched), marked with about a dozen dark-bluish spots, pectoral fin, of a yellow tinge, had thirteen rays; pelvic, nine rays, white colour; anal, nine transparent white; tail forked; fin tipped with red like the common river trout; head, particularly above the nose and eyes, of a dusky green colour, spots numerous, obscure, varying in size; gill covers silvery white, with three very distinct spots on the largest; belly and sides, up to the lateral line, silvery white, with a very few dark indistinct spots; back and sides, down to this line, dusky, inclining to green, with numerous dark spots, indistinct and varying in size. The flesh is very red, and as an article of food equalling the finest hirling. I cannot, indeed, deem it anything but a young hirling.

Five male parr-trout, average size seven inches, largest ten inches; the milt in this was large, and evidently approaching the spawning state. It was in a similar condition in one seven inches long; in the rest it resembled a thread.

Nine female parr-trout, average size seven inches long. The ova in the whole not in the slightest degree enlarged.

My principal object was to obtain parr, and I may say I fished for them alone, but took none; none of the local anglers can say they have seen any for a long time; at all events, they admit that they are not in the river at present.

CHAPTER III

LOCH LEVEN.

The angler, disposed to fish some of the waters north of the Roman wall, may start from Scotland's capital, and proceed to Kinross, in whatever way he thinks fit. If he be a true angler, he will cross the Frith of Forth to Burnt Island, and wandering westward, leave the coastline a few miles higher up. Now strike boldly to the right across a country by no means uninteresting; hilly, yet not mountainous; lonely, yet not desolate. He will traverse, it is true, no tangled forest nor copse; nor wade through wastes of blooming heather; but he will enjoy the walk notwithstanding. And now about midday, should he have crossed the Frith of Forth betimes, from the top of the high grounds, forming the southern border of the valley or basin of Leven, the lake in all its beauty and dismantled castle fills his eyes; before him and beyond, repose in solemn grandeur "the everlasting hills," whilst, at his feet, sleeps the crystal lake, gently sliding o'er its pebbly bed. But whilst his bodily eyes rest on that nature, which, though ever changing, yet ever seems the same to man, what a crowd of recollections of the past surge up before the mind's eye; of Marie Stuart, and the Douglas, and of him who drew with a master's touch the ideal panorama now flitting before the mind of the spectator.

I have a strange habit of always endeavouring to begin at the beginning. I had often visited Loch Leven, and ate its trout, but I had never fished it, and had an idea that its trout were not to be taken with an artificial fly. Experience showed this idea to be incorrect.

PRESTMANNAN

It was during a visit at Biel House, in Lothian, that I chanced to meet one good and honest angler, the late Sir Ronald Fergusson. The generous and hospitable proprietor and his lady, had invited Sir R. F. and Colonel F., Sir B. H., Lord and Lady C. myself, and several others. Four of the party, at least, were anglers; and so, next morning, we fished the artificial Lake of Prestmannan, into which, some years ago, the beauteous trout of Loch Leven had been introduced. Under circumstances highly disadvantageous, they throve, notwithstanding, tolerably well, and even bred at the entrance of a small stream which mainly supplies the lake. But what surprised me most was the being told that the trout in this pond (for the sheet of water deserves no other name) rise very readily to an artificial fly of rather larger size than is used in river fishing. In an hour, thereafter, I fished the pond; we were a *partie quarée* in two boats: General Fergusson, and Colonel Fergusson in one, Sir Benjamin Hall and I were in the other. The trout rose readily to the artificial fly as General Fergusson had told me they would; and they bit freely, so that we caught many fine trout under circumstances so adverse to the general belief as to the habits of the trout, and its natural timidity, that I could not but express my surprise thereat. Here were the fine trout, the descendants of those from Loch Leven, living in a pond, thriving and breeding, and caught so readily with an artificial fly; the angler being unassisted by wind or rain, or stream, as if by growing up in this pond they had forgotten that they were trout, whose forefathers had lived in the ample widespread waters of Leven Lake, their little ocean, with choice of food, in spring and winter, the delicate entoprostacea bringing them into the highest condition, at a season when other trout are unfit as food for man; the abundant buccinum a small whelk, but not at all microscopic, supplying them copiously during the greater part of summer, and, lastly, as a never-failing resource, flies, worms, codbait, screws, beetles, and the multifarious living things, forming the usual food of the common trout, whether he be found in lake or river.

Dinner came, and we discussed the nature of salmon and trout, and seatrout, and parr, and especially the nature of the trout now before us. I had heard and mentioned the circumstance to Sir R.F., an excellent angler and brave soldier, that in Loch Leven itself the trout could not be so caught with fly or bait. He, on the other hand, assured me that his nephews had fished Loch Leven and caught many trout. It was a question of fact, and I resolved to decide it in such a way as to leave no doubt in my own mind at least. In a week or two afterwards I was on the banks of Loch Leven.

The angler, leaving Edinburgh, will find no difficulty in reaching Kinross; the lake is at hand; as it is private property, he must engage a boat from the tenant, and in it rowing to a small rocky island towards its northern shore, he lands at the foot of that ruined castle, once the prison of Marie Stuart.

Should the wind be strong and favourable, the angler may readily enough take some good trout, as I did. The fly used was a large one, like those we used on Prestmannan Lake. It was in autumn. The trout of Loch Leven taken with nets in great numbers, to be sent all over the kingdom, and at high prices, is a beautiful, silvery, dark-spotted trout, of a species quite distinct from all river trout, and imagined by some to be peculiar to the lake. This, however, is not likely, since trout quite resembling those of Leven are found in many northern lakes. The flesh is of a fine pink colour; the eating admirable. During summer and autumn, when examined (and I have opened hundreds to ascertain the fact), the trout has its stomach filled with flies and insects, the ordinary food of the common river trout; but, in addition, it is often found to have been living on a small buccinum, or fresh-water whelk, with which the shallow waters of the lake abound.

But the great peculiarity of the trout of Loch Leven is the fact that, in December, January, and February, many Loch Leven trout come into market, and are then found to be in the highest condition; at a time when river trout are everywhere out of season and unfit for food. Curious to discover the cause of this, I examined a very great number of these winter and early spring trout. In all, I found that the food they had been living on was microscopic; that is, entomostracan, so small that the microscope was required to make out distinctly the character of the food.

These trout were in fact subsisting, thriving, and fattening on the food used by the char and the vengis, and by the herring. I am thus disposed to think that two species of trout inhabit Loch Leven, independent of the common river trout, namely, the trout which lives on entomostracæ, and comes into season in December, January, and February: and the trout, which feeding on the buccinum, and on flies, worms, and all the common food of the common river trout, comes into season much later in spring. If this view be the true one, then the early trout of Loch Leven ought to be called the char-trout, as being allied to the char in its habits and general character.

Sir Walter Scott, in his pleasant tale of the "Abbot," skilfully and naturally introduces the subject of the Leven trout, in an ideal conversation between Queen Mary Stuart and Roland Graeme. The hot-headed attendant had been, as he thought, unjustly suspected and accused. Sir Walter brings about a reconciliation in the following way: "With the peculiar tact and delicacy which no woman possessed in greater perfection, she (Queen Mary) began to soothe by degrees the vexed spirit of the magnanimous attendant. The excellence of the fish he had taken in his expedition, the high flavour and beautiful red colour of the trout which have long given distinction to the lake, led her first to express her thanks to her attendant for so agreeable an addition to her table, especially upon a *jour de jeune*; and thus brought on inquiries into the place where the fish had been taken, their size, their peculiarities; the times when they were in season, and a comparison between the Loch Leven trouts and those which are found in the rivers and lakes of the south of Scotland. The ill humour of Roland Graeme was never of an obstinate character. It rolled away like a mist before the sun, and he was easily engaged in a new and animated dissertation about Loch Leven trout, and sea trout, and river trout, and red trout, and char, which never rise to a fly, and parr, which some suppose infant salmon, and hirlings, which frequent the Frith, and vendaces, which are only found in the Castle Loch, of

Lochmaben; and he was hurrying on with the eagerness and enthusiasm of a young sportsman, when he observed" &c.

The trout of Loch Leven seem to me able to live in waters unfit for supporting the life of the river trout. This was all but proved at Prestmannan Lake. They succeed also tolerably well in an artificial lake on the property of Lady Keith, near Alloa, where I have examined them, angled for them, and taken them with the fly, late in September. In Chapter II., which describes the estuary trout, I have given the measurement of the Loch Leven trout as compared with the common trout and with that of the estuary, proving them to be specifically distinct. Other circumstances in their structure might be' added, such as the great number of the pancreatic coeca, and their great length as compared with other trout. But these are anatomical characters, merely confirmative of the natural history ones. In habits, they resemble the salmon; for in Autumn, or at the approach of Winter, they leave the lake for the streams which feed it, returning, no doubt, to the lake early in Spring. A hundred years ago, Mr. Walker pointed them out as a distinct species of trout, which all subsequent inquiries have proved to be the case. Char abounded at one time in Loch Leven, but these have disappeared. Over-fishing I imagine to be the cause. But the char also diminish in Loch Doone, where no such cause exists, in so far at least as I am aware. Char live almost exclusively on entomostraca or microscopic shellfish, like the vendace and the herring. Char prefer living in deep waters, and it may be that the repeated attempts probably to drain the lake may have succeeded in destroying the char. An amusing law process took place a few years ago respecting the fishery of this lake. No new facts were elicited in respect of the natural history of this trout. The jury, like sensible men, finding the evidence conflicting in respect of the *take of fish* which the tenant asserted had greatly fallen off in consequence of the drainage of the lake, and the want of protection to the spawning fish whilst in the feeders of the lake, arrived at a verdict in a very sensible manner. The chairman called on each of the jury to state what sum he thought might cover the loss; he next summed up the whole, and dividing by twelve, thus arrived at an average; this average they offered as their verdict: damages nearly £1000. The procedure was novel, and amused the court for some time.

I witnessed here a lamentable scene. A clever man who had followed natural history as an amateur, but was ignorant of the basis of all physiological inquiry, made statements before the court, which in fact amounted to this, that the more the lake was drained the more the trout, would thrive and multiply. Lawyers dislike science and scientific men. 1 really do not exactly know what they believe in, since to them every question has two sides. But in the case I allude to, the quasi naturalist amateur was not a scientific man but a dabbler in scientific terms. The mischief these persons have done to true science is incalculable; the more ability they have the worse it is.

Trout, and more especially as it has seemed to me the finer kinds, will live and even thrive as I have just proved, in localities apparently unsuitable for life, and where the coarsest kind, the common river trout of Scotland, for example, would surely perish. Thus, in the artificial lake in East Lothian, called Prestmannan, the Leven trout transferred to its muddy confined waters from the crystal wide-spreading Lake of Leven continue, as we have proved, to breed and to thrive tolerably well, whilst river trout soon die in the same locality.

On one occasion, it is true, about 120 dozen of these transported Leven trout floated at once to the surface, dead. I had this fact from the gamekeeper himself, who also added that he could never discover any cause for so sudden and frightful a mortality. But those which remained survived the pestilence, whatever it might be, and again restocked the pond.

No pond or lake was ever, I think, constructed on worse principles as a fishpond, than this said lake of Prestmannan, and on examining it, it occurred to me that if the Leven trout could live and thrive there, as is the case, it might do so almost anywhere.

But very fine red spotted river trout are caught in the dam head of the water of Leith, at Colt Bridge, a locality in which it is difficult to believe that any trout or fish could live, yet the fact is certain. I have moreover seen abundance of very fine red spotted trout caught in a small stream which drains the valley of Kilburne, in Derbyshire, a stream into which the refuse water of several coal pits is poured in such quantities as to blacken the entire stream. Yet but for poachers the trout in this rivulet would be numerous. They are of excellent quality. All these facts prove the practicability of greatly multiplying the amount of fine trout in Britain. To me, indeed, it seems quite practicable to stock with these fine trout most of the lakes and even ponds of Scotland, perhaps also of England. They would thrive in the Castle Loch of Lochmaben, and in most of the Highland lakes, where a trout, if not identical, at least strongly resembling that of Loch Leven, already exists.

Trout come into and go out of season not in so regular a manner as might at first be supposed. Thus the fine grey trout of Loch Leven, the trout I have ventured to call the char trout, come into season as early as December, January, and February; they are in the primest order as food for man at or soon after Christmas, and consequently at a time when all others are quite out of season and unfit for the use of man. I have caught small trout in the Whitadder as high as Priestlaw, on the 2nd February, in very good order. A heavy snowstorm overtook us whilst descending the slope of the desolate Lammermoor by Mayshiel to Spartleton, but it cleared away about eleven; the sun shone out for a brief space, and the gentle trout, small but active, rose readily to the fly. Nor do trout, as summer advances into autumn, all get out of season, although this occurs no doubt to most of them, as well male as female, the increasing of the milt giving rise to the same results on the condition of the male as that of the roe produces in the female. On these points I find amongst my notes many observations, a few of which I quote merely to authenticate the fact. The notes are simply memoranda of a few days' fishing at various times in the Gala and other rivers.

On the 20th of August, 1832, eight small trout were caught in the Gala, with the milts greatly enlarged, and advancing towards the spawning condition.

On the 24th of August, sixty trout were caught in the Whitadder; they weighed twenty pounds; of these there were thirty-nine males and twenty-one females. In twenty of the males measuring ten-and-a-half inches each, the milt was large in nineteen. In eighteen females averaging seven inches in length, the roe was small. I may here remark that the tubercle, or the extremity of the lower jaw of the male, may readily be recognised in the male of all the salmonidæ at every season; it grows to a very large size when the fish is about to deposit its spawn.

The size of the trout, at least in the Whitadder does not determine the condition of the roe and milt. I have examined trout early in September, not exceeding six inches in length, in which the ova of the roe were largely developed and actively increasing; and at the same time, on the same day, and in the same river, have taken many trout twelve or fourteen inches long, with milt and roe at their minimum. I have observed the same hold good in October. The same holds good in the salmon.

On the 25th of October, I caught some trout in Lochskene, which had been feeding on ova; this was the only occasion in which I ever detected ova in the stomach of a trout.

On the 6th of July, of sixty trout taken in some of the streams of the Whitadder at the same time, there were fifty-eight males, two females. In May, in the same river, the sexes were equal. In August, 1832, thirty-four trout taken with fly, in a feeder of the Whitadder, gave the following results:

8 male (average 9 inches)		milt very large.
5 do.		milt very small.
5 do.	(average 5 inches)	milt very large.

1 do.   milt very small.
15 females, with the ova in various conditions, but none much developed.

CHAPTER IV

THE ISLA - GLEN ISLA
"Till Birnam wood be come to Dunsinnane."

The angler, after fishing Loch Leven, should boldly stretch from Kinross to Perth, viewing in his route Abernethy's Round Tower, vestige of an unknown antiquity, exciting in the beholder a mysterious awe. How singularly has human history been written, and how widely different in their intellectual natures must be the men who now live from those that were. We cannot even guess at the purpose of their grandest architectural works, nor the date of their erection.

O' Beirne is dead, who wrote, or rather guessed at, the history of these towers. But that book of his explains not why these towers occur chiefly in Ireland, two only in Scotland, and none in England. They are to be found, it is said, in Persia, but I know not who vouches for this. We Westerns comprehend not at all the myths of the Eastern world. Barbarous, vulgar, unimaginative West! Beer-swilling, heavy-carcased Scandinavians! in what time could you have invented a pyramid, a temple, an obelisk? Or even you flat-nosed Franks, who have more of soul, more of the transcendental within you, even you came not quite up to the Oriental. So says the author of "Tancred." But I will tell you what you have, and what his race has not; a slight love of truth in ordinary life; some regard for truth in history; a deep feeling for truth in science. With you, Orientals, truth in chronology has no meaning. The earth with you is a plain; the sun, moon, stars, and planets frisk around it, having been made for it. Even money, which men say we Franks and Scandinavians worship as a god, does not with us represent everything, take the place of everything, as with that race who, whether on Sinai or on Highgate, in Jerusalem or in St. Mary Axe, are always the same.

The angler will make for Perth, no doubt, and soon for Dunkeld; but before doing so, I recommend him to look at the Tay, at Kinfauns, and, crossing it, then proceed at once to

Newtyle, and from this point fish the Isla; he will find excellent streams near the bridge, above and below. The trout resemble the English trout; they are red-spotted, excellent to eat, and of a pale rose colour when opened up. There are others, no doubt, of the common sorts, and parrs abound. Seatrout and salmon appear in their proper season, and much of the ground is open. Other streams exist higher up, but 1 did not fish them. The natives are primitive, and the slopes of Glen Isla healthy, no doubt, to strangers; but nowhere have I seen more disease than in the inhabitants of these original looking villages and detached cottages. The morale beats Paris all to nothing; but in other respects, they are a Sabbath observing population, devout, full of faith, and of large professions. Like the common people of all countries, they are profoundly ignorant of everything around them. Of the past of their own country they know nothing; of the present but little. I inquired of one of the oldest of these cottar-farmers what mountains those were in the distance He did not know. I knew them to be the Grampians. Of Macbeth he had never heard, but knew a report that a long time ago there lived a great giant in a cave on Dunsinnane hill! Such is "la peuple."

Whilst angling in this valley, the kind-hearted proprietor of Dunsinnane invited me to visit the mansion he occupied, and which also belonged to him, together with the surrounding estate, stands on the western side of the valley, opposite "high Dunsinnane." It is a wooded valley, terminating in the vale of the Tay.

As I stood with Mr. Nairne on Dunsinnane hill, it occurred to me that the person who wrote the Macbeth of Shakespere must have been here in person. Mr. N., a brave and experienced officer, concurred with me, that the writer of the tragedy must not only have been on the spot, but viewed the ground with a military eye. It is on Dunsinnane that you command a full view of the entire valley, as far as Birnam Wood. In this wood alone could an army have lain concealed, so as not to be discovered from Dunsinnane; and here Shakespere places the Scoto-English force under Macduff and Seward:

> "Till Birnam wood be come to Dunsinnane I
> shall not move:
> And now, behold, the wood begins to move."

Thou master of the human mind, how admirably hast thou laid the plot of Macbeth! Nothing escaped your genius, neither place nor circumstance. The Celtic mind, as well as that of the lowland Scot, was known to you; you knew its strength and foible. The weird sisters; the bare and blasted heath, shine out more clearly in your pages than in the paintings of Zucharelli. In your grand artistic sketch the living actors are before us. Immortal Shakespere! First of poets. "Macbeth, a Tragedy," would have secured everlasting renown to any name.

Higher up the valley there stands a noble castle, called Glamis Castle. It well deserves a visit; and so also does Dunkeld, where the Tay itself and many noble streams may be angled in. I have not fished these waters myself, but I believe them to be good. A longer rod will be required than for the streams I have spoken of; good tackle and choice flies and minnows. The great proprietor here is the Duke of Atholl, who is uniformly polite to the well-bred.

On one occasion on my way to Taymouth I revisited Dunkeld. A friend drove me in his gig from Perth to Dunkeld, whence I left on foot for Aberfeldie, passing on my way Grand Tully, where I might have halted; but for Sir John, whom I knew was dead, and Sir William in other lands. On taking up my evening quarters at the Breadalbane Arms of Aberfeldie, I was startled at some unearthly noises which ill-accorded with a highland inn. A stamping and yelling; a rushing out and a rushing in; a banging to of doors; a sort of leaping and dancing on the naked floors—to crown all, someone played a fiddle horribly out of tune. Startled I was, but said nothing until next morning, when the whole secret came out. Some eighteen or twenty Cambridge Bricks were passing their vacation here, with their tutor. True to their Saxon nature, and being at the same time thorough bricks, they were never at rest for an instant; they talked very loudly; scoured the village in troops some twenty times a day; dressed fantastically, some in the tartan and philabeg; their thin and fleshless English shanks were indescribably comic, and I laughed until I nearly dropped. But that which most amused me was, that they fancied they were "doing the highlander." Never did I see the races of men so well contrasted. The calm, polite, soft-speaking Celt; the stormy, noisy, boorish, roaring, fretful Saxon.

As next morning I walked towards the Castle, expecting to hear from its noble proprietor, who at the time was in Argyleshire, I mused much on what I had seen. I knew "the bricks" well, and had often seen them before, but I had never met them previously so much out of their beat. On the banks of the Cam or at the Clarendon, over a bottle of good port, they look quite at home; but here, in the land of the Gael, alas!

The streams which feed Loch Tay are open, I think, to the angler, for their noble proprietor is generous, hospitable, and free. But I did not fish them on my first visit some years ago, being otherwise engaged with lake fishing, grouse shooting, and climbing Ben Lawers. I advise the angler to avoid all these amusements; mountain climbing I have ever found to be a most unprofitable business, although I am aware that in skilful hands who know how to ring the changes dexterously on bells, which have been often played, a mountain ascent is by no means an unprofitable speculation.

Kenmore must be a pretty good trouting station, and so also is Aberfeldie. But I speak not from personal experience. From Kenmore the angler may make for the Erne, or returning to Taymouth Cross, the mountainous pass of Loch Turits Glen: or returning to Aberfeldie as I did, strike across the country by the Black House of Balfracks, and so reach Dunkeld by Glen Braun. He will require a guide.

The red-spotted, pink-coloured trout of the Isla, and of some other Scottish streams to which I have already alluded, are at least analogous to those of England, and may even be identical as to species. But this I will not affirm. I have seen such trout caught in the streams of Derbyshire, into which the muddy coal-black water runs which was being discharged from extensive coal fields, and in situations in which I had scarcely thought it possible for trout or any other sort of fish to live; yet they not only lived but throve admirably in these streams, and were excellent to eat.

I have not fished the Hampshire streams nor those which form the Thames, but I have examined many trout from Hampshire and Oxford. In one from Hampshire, which measured $14\frac{1}{2}$ inches, the gape was $1\frac{5}{8}$, and the length of the head $3\frac{1}{2}$ inches. There were two of these trout; the one selected for me by Mr. Groves (he looks to shape and form) measured 16 inches. Red and black spots abounded. This was on the 11th of June. Fine trout are caught in the Stour, which runs by Canterbury, and many Kentish streams are noted for good trout. The trout of the south of England seem to me excellent, being generally pink-coloured in the flesh; those of the north, and more especially the trout of the Coquet, resemble the common river trout of Scotland; they amuse the angler, but are worthless for the table.

CHAPTER V

LOCH KATRINE – VENACHER – FINLAS

Mental fatigue and bodily toil, carpeted rooms, dining in and dining out, but, worst of all, the commonplace of a large city, had done its best and its worst to drive from my mind and body all thought and energy. So I said to my friend, this can be endured no longer, and next morning by break of day we were off to Stirling.

The angler may reach Stirling as he chooses; on foot, by rail, by coach or horse, by steamboat. I recommend the last mode as the pleasantest, though tedious. The boat will carry him up the Forth, along its winding bank; its link; the rich carse of Falkirk is passed through on the one hand; on the other, the Ochils, a range of beautiful hills, behind which runs the Devon, but I never fished the Devon, although I am aware that the scenery on its banks is most beautiful, and it presents in its upper waters, like the Clyde, a proof that the fish, called parr, is somehow or other connected with the salmon, and for the same reason, namely, that at one part of its course a fall exists too high for the salmon to overleap.

Let us return to the Forth.

As we sailed briskly along, chatting pleasantly with various friends, whom you are almost sure to meet on the deck of a steamboat, time passed agreeably enough. Someone or other knows the coast, the hills, the mansions, the people. We met an old schoolfellow, a most worthy man, now a lawyer, and in office. Amongst various things we talked off, he put this odd question to me -Why is it now that recruiting officers are directed to look at the form and appearance of the hands of all offering themselves as recruits? I explained to him that without pretending to know the precise reason, or all the reasons for such an order, there still were some obvious enough; such as the size of the hands of the recruits, which, if small, unfitted the recruit from readily handling his musket; and again, a small hand implies a luxurious disposition and a dislike to continued labour, the *"labor improbus,"* which overcomes all things. As we conversed, I used my own hand as a demonstration of some points of our discourse; he put forward his also, but instantly drew it back in consternation. He had never looked at his hand before. Like many human hands it was scarcely human; long, muscular, spatular-shaped fingers; vast breadth of palm, thumb-joint and other joints standing out at right angles; nails indescribable. He saw the whole at a glance. And now followed a discourse on form and on beauty, which carried us back to the glorious age of Greece, opened up a new world to the vision of my friend, who then learned what neither Blackstone nor Coke upon Lyttleton could have taught him, the laws, namely, which regulate the formation and the deformation of the human form; of the absolutely beautiful and the conventionally so.

By this time we had reached Stirling, and at once took to the road for Callender, eschewing all coaches, horses, and gigs. But marching through a level fertile country does not restore the energy of the body and elasticity of mind, which a bold sally through a mountain district temporarily does. The high road, too, savours too much of a town—of commonplace Highgate, Hammersmith, and the Borough. But the angler must not mind this; so we marched onwards, reaching Cullender that evening. Slow work this, on a September day, but one intensely hot, and so we were fain to rest there for the evening.

Our road, early next morning, lay along the banks of Loch Venachar, abounding, as we were told, with fine brown trout; but the lake belongs to somebody who now represents Rhoderick Dhu in this quarter, and whose permission it is necessary to have, in order to fish its waters. The scenery on its banks is tame, the road without interest, save that doubtful notoriety bestowed on it by the genius whose fame suffered so severely by his unhappy poetry, if it deserve the name. We are approaching the country of the Gael -nay, we are in it. Coilintogle ford is in sight on the left:

so is Loch Venachar. The morning is beautiful. Rounding the mountains on the right, the bridge of Turk comes into view, beyond which followed

> "The copsewood grey,
>> That wooed and wept on Loch Achray."

The angler will find a lodging at the bridge of Turk, and another at the entrance of Glenfinlas. We preferred the latter.

The MacGregors are not far off, the descendants of Rob Roy. They are fine-looking men, but have blue eyes.

Our next care was to look out for angling-ground. Before us lay the small stream running from Loch Achray to Venachar. I fished it with the utmost care, but unsuccessfully. The waters, it is true, were low, the sun bright, and the pools unruffled. I could not learn that the fishing was ever successful in this connecting stream, or that any of the brown trout ascended it from Venachar, or descended it from Loch Achray, and yet at times this must be the case, as in floods; for trout run madly up a flooded stream, and may then be taken in dozens by the veriest bungler; no skill is required then.

Unsuccessful in the stream, I now fished the river, which, to the south of the Trosachs, connects Loch Katrine with Loch Achray. To reach this stream, you walk from the Bridge of Turk, then along the beautiful banks of Loch Achray, and, passing the inn built in the gorge of the Trosachs, turn to the left, cross the river " that joins Loch Katrine to Loch Achray," close to the mill, and proceed upwards until reaching the smooth gravelly shore of the lake, Benvenue stands full before you; precipitous and wild, stopping all progress on that side the lake. Now look to the north and east, the Trosachs are spread out before you, a wild, rocky, and tangled scene, well suited for an ambuscade, even now. You must not feel displeased that the scenery falls far short of the jingling description of poor Sir Walter. The bold cliffs of Benvenue, this lone lake's western boundary, cannot be injured by description.

On this classic ground—for classic it is, perhaps—I now stood. It was mid-day:

> "All in the Trosach's glen was still:
> Noontide was sleeping on the hill."

The stream is short, difficult to fish, but there is no lack of good common trout. I saw none of the brown trout of the lake (Loch Katrine), which I heard of as being mostly disposed of by a Highland gentleman angler to the innkeeper at Achray. All persons who live without working are esteemed to be gentlemen by the Gael. Angling is not working; it is an amusement. A person who lives by angling is a gentleman; he toils not, neither does he spin; with the never-ready, ever-late race, he is therefore a gentleman.

I descended the stream, fishing it as carefully as I could. At certain times there must be splendid sport here. But the stream is difficult to fish, and extremely rocky, It runs through the Trosachs, in fact, on the southern side; another stream, but smaller, passes through on the other side. I did not see it. The day was bright and warm. I recommend the angler to try the stream I fished, when flooded, early in the morning: he can easily get there before the Gael, who will have his tackle to find and his rod to mend when they are wanted, although he knew all this a month ago. When a boat is required in the land of the Gael, it is then remembered that the hole in the side, made two months since, had not been closed. When this is done, an oar, broken long ago, has still to be repaired; the tiller is not to be found, it having been used for fire-wood, or to mend a stable door. This is the Gael.

I turned my back on Loch Katrine and Loch Achray, perhaps to see them no more. The pure air of these mountains and lakes had in a few days restored me to health and strength. I began again to feel like a man, and not like a cit: Piccadilly and the clubs; the Haymarket and its snobs; hard, dry, flinty iron-bound Trafalgar-square, were utterly forgotten. I now felt sufficiently strong to attempt Glenfinlas.

A lovely far-winding glen, commencing by a wooded gorge, a waterfall and a rushing stream, leads from the bridge of Turk towards the north and east. This is the bed of the Finlas. As you ascend the Highland glen, the woods gradually disappear and meadows of no great width take their place. On these the sheep farmers were busy collecting their winter fodder for the numerous flocks of sheep which browsed the lofty mountains shutting in the glen. We ascended it for miles, until, the stream becoming small, it was thought advisable to try our fortune with the finny brood.

I fished it from this spot to where, rushing into the wooded gorge, angling was impracticable. The Finlas is a good stream. Salmon ascend it as high at least as the falls. I do not recollect whether they pass the fall or not, but I almost think they do; for the fall is more a succession of short rapids than a fall. Besides, at the bridge of Turk, the angler may have some good sport in the Finlas, and at a trifling expense try his fortune on Loch Katrine.

It was the opinion I think, of the sagacious Sancho—sagacious as a dog, or a weasel, or a pig, to which animal he bore in habits a near resemblance—that one must live long to see much. I had always thought that no such person was to be found as a female athlete; but there lived at the time I speak of, at the bridge of Turk, a hostess, who came as near the character of an athlete as anyone I ever beheld. Still, to complete the character of a prize-fighter, there was wanting the bold brow, the look of defiance, the enormous neck and brawny limbs. Yet, she was, I was assured, a terrible woman in her way, and talked familiarly about the number of men she had knocked down—including her husband, of course. I did not venture to try her strength in any way.

And now threading our way by Venachar and Callender, in a single bold march we reached Stirling, and by eventide were passing Number 39, in the Castle-street of Edinburgh, where the author of the "Lady of the Lake" passed so many happy and so many anxious days. Farewell to the Land of the Mist!

Savage Maculloch! what could induce you so to maltreat the unhappy Gael? Voltaire, it is true, handled them sharply enough; he knew them well; read his Lettres aux Velsches." But the instrument he used was a fine-edged Damascus blade your weapon, a thing compounded of the geological hammer, with which you fractured the rocks of their mountains, and a tomahawk. It was well for you that you did not revisit the Highlands; had they but caught you on the quay of Greenock, they would have "pruised you like a pinch of snuff."

The Gael whom you so abused now flees his country; he must leave; his doom has come; his destiny is determined. He flees before the Saxon butcher the red deer and the grouse will dislodge his tiny sheep and cattle. Queen Anne said that she would turn Scotland into a hunting-field; she must have meant Caledonia. A very common mistake of both queens and subjects is the confounding Scotland with Caledonia—Scottishmen with Celts. Sam Johnson did it, and so do most people, especially the English. But these countries are very, very distinct.

Caledonia may soon become a great hunting-field; its name blotted from out the history of nations. It never was a nation, any more than New Zealand, but a wild land, inhabited by savage tribes of men, whose pastime was bloodshed, violence, robbery. Yet the "Lady of the Lake" of Scott, and the "Donna di Lago" of the great maestro, may live long in the memory of men.

CHAPTER VI

THE DOONE; LOCH DOONE; THE LOCH OF KEN
"Before him Doone
Pours all his floods." —BURNS.

The angler who is desirous of fishing these waters should proceed to Ayr, making that ancient town his headquarters. I travelled from Castle Cary in a gig, by a road we had not previously journeyed, our object being to see the river Ayr as near its source as we well could. Our road lay, in fact, to Mauchline, which, though famed "For honest men and bonnie lassies," is not a place for anglers. After a drive over a dreary and un interesting country, we reached the town in which the immortal Burns passed some of the happiest days of his life; but for his memory, the place is not worth naming, nor looking at, and so next morning a short walk brought us to the wooded banks of the Ayr. Wild, rocky, and tangled with trees and bushes, the river forms a succession of short streams and deep still pools, which no winds can touch. It was a warm autumn morning, and the still water resembled molten glass—a polished mirror, reflecting strongly and deeply each tree, and rock, and passing cloud. I was not prepared for meeting so wild a scene; it must have aided Burns' inspiration, but he has nowhere alluded to it.

The difficulty of reaching the margin of the stream was considerable; the pools deep and dangerous; it was all but impossible to angle. Lower down, however, I think we did take a few small trout, but the Ayr at this point is clearly not a trouting stream; so we descended its banks until, reaching a small roadside inn, close to Stair, we breakfasted luxuriously on tea and kippered salmon, and, returning to Mauchline, proceeded at once by the banks of the Ayr to the town itself. It was a long drive. I recommend all anglers to avoid the Ayr; its banks are beset with weavers' villages, who, no doubt, clear its waters of every living trout, salmon, or sea trout, as fast as they appear. On seeing these villages, we drove on; it was quite enough; and, as the sun descended on the western ocean, we found a resting place not far from "the Wallace Tower."

The next day we examined the mouth of the Doone, looking out for angling ground. We had an opportunity of examining the fishing baskets of two young anglers who had been fishing in the lowest pools of bonnie Doone. They contained nothing but parr. A walk to Alloa kirk and the bridge of Doone, that bridge which Tam O'Shanter has made immortal, showed me that there was no angling of moment in the lower stream of the Doone; so, after gazing for a while on a somewhat fantastic, misplaced monument, erected here in memory of him who requires no monument, and looked at that stream in which Tam's wife foretold that he would someday be found, "deep drowned in Doone," and at the bridge and haunted kirk, which will live in the memory of man for countless ages, we turned our horse's head towards Dalmellington.

The road to Dalmellington runs along the banks of the Doone. An angler might, I think, walk this road with advantage. The Doone is at hand; he walks along those banks and braes so celebrated in song; they are pretty, but in no way remarkable. I should not think the Doone much of an angling river in any part of its course; but it is frequented by salmon which reach by its means Loch Doone itself.

On clearing the wooded banks of the Doone, you stand at once at the source of the river, and on the margin of as desolate and wild a lake as fancy can well picture. The Eagles' Crag, bold, precipitous, dark, and frowning, rises to a great height beyond the lake, whilst all around huge heather-clad mountains shut in the waste of waters. Towards the eastern extremity of the lake is a small island, on which stand the ruins of an ancient castle of great strength.

We had two guides with us; not that you absolutely require any guides to reach the banks of the lake, but you cannot well fish it but from a boat, at least with any chance of success. From them we derived a good' deal of information; and first, of course, they allowed me to use my own flies, at the same time assuring me that we should catch no fish; and this happened, although I used the best, large and small, and those especially I had found so successful in rivers. They next recommended me to try some of their dressing: large gaudy flies, dressed in gay colours, with silver finishings. I had never seen such an artificial fly before; nevertheless, we succeeded perfectly, and in a short time caught a good basket of trout.

These were of two kinds apparently; none, were large; a few are found in the lake, although I do not remember taking any; and char, which rise not at a fly," exist also in Loch Doone. Of these we, of course, saw nothing. A large salmon rose at the fly, but did not bite. The char and salmon no doubt breed in the lanes which connect Loch Enoch just under the Eagles' Crag with Loch Doone. This Loch Enoch must be the wildest spot in Scotland. I regret not having visited it.

We saw no large trout, neither do I think that such are common; nevertheless, I speak from a brief experience. It should be tried with parr-tail and minnow, and with salmon flies of various kinds. The shores are rocky, barren, and desolate beyond imagination. A savage country, without a road or hope of civilization.

Should any angler, fond of nature, visit the ground I have just described, I venture to recommend him first to visit Loch Enoch, and, returning to Dalmellington, journey from thence by the Loch of Ken to Kirkcudbright, and from that ancient and primitive burgh, he may explore with success the wilds of Galloway. Small lakes scattered over that desolate region are said to contain pink-coloured trout of exquisite flavour. I visited by this route Kirkcudbright, but did not fish the Dee, a good salmon river, whose chief source is Loch Ken. My object was different. I desired to see the birthplace of most of my family; to gaze on St. Mary's Isle, of which I had heard so much in my youth; and on Selkirk Hall," plundered by Paul Jones, of which said invasion my friends were eye-witnesses:

ADMIRAL JOHN PAUL JONES.

Ye've heard of Paul Jones,

Have ye not, have ye not?
We've heard of Paul Jones,
Have ye not, have ye not?
Ye've heard of Paul Jones, BORDER SONG

JOURNEY TO THE SOLWAY FROM DALMELLINGTON BY THE LOCH OF KEN.

On a soft autumnal day, such as rarely occurs in Scotland, my good grey mare and gig were ordered to be ready betimes in the morning. My companion and I (anglers should have no companions) were preparing to leave Dalmellington, where we had been residing for some days; we had fished Loch Doone; gazed at the Eagles' Crag; scanned from the heights the wildest part of Ayrshire; to all this, I said, we shall return some day; let us, in the meantime, visit the Loch of Ken, St. Mary's Isle, and the desolate shores of the stormy Solway. A true angler, I am persuaded, must be born such; he cannot become so by education. There is no education in it—it is all romance. A love of the lovely, the wild and solitary, characterize the northern angler; with him the purple heath, the ruined castle, the melancholy bleating of the innocent sheep, the solemn stillness of the heath-clad desert, the deep cauldron linn and stream, pure as the crystal, as it leaps and rushes down rocky wooded dells, are objects in the contemplation of which he never wearies. With him, there is no ennui, whether he climb the Cheviot or his path lie by Tweed's calmer and classic banks: Tweed, famed in song and story, sung and told by those now numbered with the dead.

Our way lay eastward. Magic word! eastward! Why is it that we love to travel towards the east? Freedom moves westward, and has done so for ages. Do men follow the sun in pursuit of the real, and salute his rising when longing for the ideal? Hope turns us towards the east; reality to the west. But let us journey onwards, lest we reach not the Solway before the setting rays of that bright orb, the god of this lower world, shall have gilded the summits of the Eagles' Crag, which is still in view. And now, journeying slowly along, the huge and massive Carsphairn rises on our left, stony and steep, unprofitable, nor yet romantic; without an Alpine character, you yet look as if you had been, for ever and for ever, one of the foundations of the earth!

I have angled now for half a century, yet nature seems to me for ever the same; nor time nor circumstance, science nor philosophy, have ever affected my love of nature; to efface it seems impossible. All may be vanity and vexation of spirit with those over whose minds conventionalism holds its flickering, trifling, soul-destroying, levelling sway; but all is not vanity with me. The fibre touched by the absolutely true, the perfect, the beautiful, the universal, is still as fresh as when a boy I wandered by the banks of the Whitwater, or climbing desolate Minch Moor first caught sight of Yarrow's flooded stream, or roamed by the banks of the Seine, or gazed listlessly from the slopes of the Anatolo. Why should we weary or become tired of nature? Is the sun less bright? Has the mountain-top lost its aerial tints? the moon her silvery lustre? the lake its molten glassy surface? and should the work before us be not of nature but of human hands, yet, absolutely perfect and beautiful, does it sink into odious commonplace? Do we tire of gazing at the Venus, the Apollo, the Diana, the Minerva? Never! What fills us with ennui, with satiety, is the so-called nature of civilized man; the nature as fashioned by the citizen, the utilitarian, the man of the day. Everything he does smacks of the shop, the counter, the banker's book, the means and end. Poetasters, versifiers, colourists, men of dodges and tricks! your clumsy deceptions will pass away whether attempted on canvas, in marble, in gardening, in architecture; it will all pass away like yourselves; but Nature, ever young, ever fresh, ever beautiful, will still remain, and with her those immortal names who have seen her face to face. The Cena of Leonardo will never pall on human minds.

I had brought my angler to Carsphairn; a well made carriage-road led thence to the high grounds overlooking the Loch of Ken. We visited not its immediate banks, but journeying onwards, gained the point where a ferry pointed out to us the necessity of deciding on our future course. Two roads lay before us; by crossing the ferry we might shorten our route to Kirkcudbright, which was to be our resting-place, if possible, for the evening. But we learned that the road was wild, somewhat difficult, traversing the most uncultivated parts of Galloway; inns scarce; accommodation for man and horse difficult to be obtained; the sun had crossed the high lands of Galloway; the valley of the lake was already becoming obscure. Yet it was by this road we hesitated travelling, that Robert Burns journeyed on horseback when on a visit to the noble family of Selkirk. On that wild and desolate heath he composed that immortal ode, the Song of Liberty.

But there was another inducement to travel by this road which, yet strong as it was, prevailed not. A young friend, a native himself of these wilds, had assured me that there lay scattered over that mountain range or country, small lakes, containing trout of estimable quality; dark-spotted, of moderate size, pink. coloured flesh, admirable to eat. Now I am fond of trout with pink-coloured flesh. On reading this, some will affirm that I cannot be a true sportsman. Nor am I; I never viewed as a sport the destruction of any animal. I wander by the banks of lake and river, trying here and trying there, careless what be the success or result. Latterly, I confess, my ideas on this point occasionally underwent a change, the cause of which shall appear in the sequel of this journey.

Prudence prevailed, and we turned our horse's head towards Castle Douglas, keeping therefore along the northern side of Ken for many miles. And now it was nightfall, and we had to .inquire our way of the first traveller we met. He proved to be a friend and old acquaintance; a short half-hour brought us to Castle Douglas. How we sped there, I need not relate. The town happened to be full of personal and esteemed friends, of whose residence I was ignorant at the time. But declining all their kind invitations, we left by break of day this friendly and pleasant town, making our way with all convenient speed to Kirkcudbright. Of that which I have neither seen nor touched, I can form no sure idea, neither did I ever meet with anyone who could. Yet never was I accused of a defective imagination. St. Mary's Isle, Kirkcudbright, the Loch of Ken, and Paul Jones, were as familiar to me as household words. They were household words. From the time I could listen to anything, the first words I heard were, St. Mary's Isle, the Mill and the Miller of Dee, and Paul Jones. Coupled with these were romantic stories, yet narrated to me as true, and which, could I relate them as told, were unquestionably true. But the events I speak of happened before my time, and yet were fresh in the recollection of the much-beloved person who narrated them to me. It seemed that on a time, the time I now speak of, my friends held a farm of the family of Selkirk. The Little Mote, I think, was the name I often heard it called by, but when I visited Kirkcudbright no such place could be found. There stood, it is true, a homestead or farmhouse, or barn, and a few labouring peasants occupied a cottage near. From the presence of a marl-pit at hand, I conjectured that this must be the spot where brothers and sisters now dead and gone first saw the light; and the adjoining height was the mote; but all had been enclosed in the park and home farm of the noble owner; and as I had not come there to trace the site of a ruined farm-house, I soon abandoned the inquiry. But returning to the times when my father held a farm in this .locality, it is sufficient to say, that they were the times of Paul Jones' visit to St. Mary's Isle. How he landed there, the Bonhomme Riehard tacking off and on in the Solway a few miles distant; how he took possession of the house of the earl, who, fortunately for himself, happened to be in London, or at least from home; how he dined with the countess and her friends, removing, however, after dinner, all the plate; all this has been told by others; . but I heard the story from the lips of one who was present at the dreaded meeting. How this plate was afterwards sold in France, the money divided amongst his crew, the plate repurchased by Paul Jones, and presented to the countess, I have heard from the same lips the romance, for such it really was, with certain anecdotes which have escaped, I think, the grubbing collectors of *anas*, the Boswells of the day. Of these little incidents I shall relate but one. When the boats of the Bonhomme Richard withdrew from the Dee, night began to fall, and the townsmen, who had very prudently kept out of the way, showed themselves in some force. They had discovered a cannon somewhere that they could not find before, and having made this discovery it was easy enough to find something to fire at. As night fell, they saw a dark mass looming in the distance some way down the river. It could be nothing else but the boats of the spoliator returning with the crew to sack the town. They manfully fired the cannon, when suddenly on their left, the report was repeated; again it boomed, once, twice, thrice; they v,ᶜere going to be surrounded and massacred. Sudden as lightning the gallant townsmen fled, abandoning gun and town, mansion and lady, wives and children. But morning dawned; the cannon vvʸas where they had left it; what they took for boats was a rock, an object they might have seen every day of their lives; the cannonading they had heard was the report of their own gun, repeated ten times by echo. It was a bitter. joke, which I have been told none who were parties to the sham fight, but real flight, choose to hear spoken of.

When Lord Selkirk returned and found the plate gone, he stormed and swore that had he been but present, he would have ate up Paul Jones and his crew! Poor man! I have heard that he had more courage than sense; very likely but he must also have been witty, for whilst on the subject of the plate, he hinted to his lady that her ladyship ought rather to have presented Paul Jones with her own dowry. Witty, but severe; and somewhat unmanly. Lady Selkirk was most beautiful; but at the same time a portionless lass with a long pedigree.

Our search after the little mote being unsuccessful, we returned to the inn, and to the town and river. They were taking salmon with stage-nets, a mode of fishing I had never seen before; we had some for breakfast. There is no trout fishing here; the banks of the river are low, muddy, influenced by the tide. The people had an outlandish, half-Celtic look; they call themselves Gallowegians. The goldfinch is found here, indicating a mild and sheltered spot. I imagine the town to be a finished town. On the western bank of the river were pointed out to me the lands of Mr. Broughton Murray, of whom I had heard much.

The salmon we saw taken were not of large size; of trout, we saw none. In the stream below the mill, I have no doubt they abound, and the river up to Loch Ken has unquestionably its finny brood; but I did not explore it, and cannot advise. I should not think this an angling country; and this being our opinion at the time, we prepared to quit on the same day the " Isle" with all its recollections, intending to reach the shores of the Solway by another route.

The redoubted Paul Jones, whose real name however was John Paul Jones, the Nelson of his day, was, as I have been assured, a native of Kirkcudbright. Whilst a boy, and in Lord Selkirk's service, he was struck by the earl, which blow he never forgot nor forgave. His true history has probably never yet been written. His was a life of romance. The Gallowegians, disliking his memory, and smarting perhaps under their own discomfiture, have recorded his visit or visitation in some doggerel rhymes which I have often heard sung by a native of Galloway, of which I have already quoted a verse; here are some more:

> Ye've heard of Paul Jones,
> > Have ye not, have ye not?
> Ye've heard of Paul Jones,
> > Have ye not, have ye not?
> Ye've heard of Paul Jones,
> > Who was a rogue and a vagabones.
> Ye've heard of Paul Jones,
> > Have ye not, have ye not?
> How he came to Selkirk Hall,
> > Did he not, did he not? How he
> came to Selkirk Hall,
> > Did he not, did he not?
> How he came to Selkirk Hall And
> > stole the jewels all,
> > And stole the jewels all,
> > > Have ye not, have ye not!
> He was a murderer,
> > Was he not, was he not!
> He was a murderer,
> > Was he not, was he not!

> For on board a man-of-war
>   He slew his carpenter,
>   He slew his carpenter,
>   Did he not, did he not?

The English of that day have succeeded in classing Paul Jones with pirates and buccaneers! an excellent device. When you cannot beat an enemy, be sure to slander him. They tried the same plan with Napoleon, but it did not take. Falsehoods well timed serve a purpose, but they are sure to rebound sooner or later on the heads of their inventors.

CHAPTER VII

THE NITH AND ITS TRIBUTARIES

"As wandering by Nith I wait the dewy eve."

BURNS.

I have not a very high opinion of the Nith and its tributaries as angling streams. The population on its banks is too dense, the villages too numerous, weavers and other mechanics too abundant. Still these streams are worth a visit by the angler, who, finding himself in Dumfries, may feel a melancholy pleasure in wandering by the banks of the river, where mused the immortal lyric bard of Scotland. On Nith-side was he last seen angling. His mind had evidently become disturbed. I do not infer this from his having been found angling, but from the guise in which he showed himself. He wore a huge hairy cap, and had girded on an old rusty claymore. Thus was he last seen on the banks of the Nith. Alas!

The angler will find the best station for fishing the upper waters of the Nith, as I shall venture to call them, at the village of Keir, about ten miles from Dumfries. From this he may fish the Nith itself, and two or three of the streams which join it from the south. In one of these—Carn, I think—a soft and gently flowing stream, running to the south of Ken, through a stiff, loamy, slimy, pipe-clay soil, he will find a peculiar kind of trout—at least as to external appearances; but it is thirty years since I saw it, and cannot speak now with certainty. In the Nith, unless aided by weather and floods, he will catch nothing but parr, which the people about Drumlanrig mistake for young salmon, and the usual river trout, red-spotted and small. But it must be different at other times, when autumnal floods run high; for hirling and sea trout, and salmon, and bull trout ascend the Nith in considerable numbers, despite the mms and mill-dam of Dumfries.

This is the country of the treacherous and bloody Kirkpatricks —not of Closeburn, for Closeburn does not, nor ever did, belong to them, but to one of the kindest and most hospitable of families, Menteith of Closeburn. Drumlanrig once boasted of its breed of wild cattle, but these, I think, have been destroyed, or suffered to become extinct. Fish the Nith, and a strong stream which joins it from the south and west, and, crossing the ridge of hills to the south of Keir, fish the Carn: it will lead you to Dumfries.

LOWER WATERS OF THE NITH

I never fished these waters; nor did I ever see anyone angling in them. The river is here fished with the net, as the fishing belongs to the town of Dumfries. But for this it would, I think, furnish sport to the angler, but have some doubts as to this, for throughout the greater part of its course it is influenced by the tide. Nevertheless, it abounds with the salmonidæ, and it may interest the angler to hear them described as I saw them, taken with the net.

I left the angler at Kirkcudbright, on the Dee; and from this we started for Dumfries.

I am persuaded that no true angler ever - unless compelled so to do by force of circumstances—travels to the field of his enjoyment on horseback, in a gig or chariot, in a post-chaise, or by the most frightful and most odious of all means of conveyance, the rail. The angler leaves his home as old Izaak did, if allowed to do so, on foot, using the instruments of travel which Nature has bestowed on him. He is, or ought to be, a simpleminded man; no jolly-good-dinner fellow; no roysterer; no hack *littérateur*; no uproarious bully; no clubbist; no man in search of the picturesque—that is, Saxon burlesque, the mock sentimental. Such men have angled, and written about angling, and they may have written well about it, just as the man of no feeling best described "The Man of Feeling." But anglers such persons are not; they are roysterers and bullies, who seek the water-side as a relief from dissipation. The poor Cockney, who travels to the Tweed in a post-chaise, and appears soon after on its quiet placid bank, cased, like Hamlet's ghost, in furs and waterproofs sufficient to carry him harmless to the pole: even he, though no angler, is a better sort of creature than the roystering roaring bully type, of whom I have seen several. They haunted Inverleithen, and were the pest of that sweet spot.

A superior class, usually fox-hunters, infested, and perhaps still infest, the Cross Keys, Kelso. None such are true anglers. But be this as it may, time and tide wait for no man, and so we left the Dee by the same conveyance which brought us there—namely, a gig, drawn by my good grey mare, making our way, without loss of time, towards Dumfries. Man and horse require food, and so we rested at a village or town which the traveller will find about half way between Kirkcudbright and the capital of Dumfriesshire, Dumfries—of some celebrity, chiefly for the cruel fate of the poet Burns; Burns, who gauged beer-barrels, whilst George the Third sat on the throne of England. "And what for no?" as the landlady of the Cleikum Inn says, in "St. Ronan's Well,"—"what for no" As you sow, so must You reap: your social system leads to this; based on self, it can only end in selfish results. Men of genius are of necessity trodden down amidst the universal rush for gold. When gold alone is esteemed, valued, worshipped, all other things must sink in value; and this reminds me of one of the bully type, who also gave himself out for an angler, affirming that he never yet met a patriotic, public-minded man, a philanthropist, who was not at the same time a scoundrel! This man, though a good mechanical angler, was of the Satanic school. Let us leave him to his own reflections, and proceed on our journey.

The town or village we now reached wore a curious foreign aspect; I fancied it had a Flemish air; a something monkish about it; a physiognomy unlooked-for in Protestant and protesting Scotland; on inquiry, we found out that it really was the seat of a nunnery, or monkery, or some such establishment, and that I had not been deceived in my first glance of the place. Important, most important, are the first impressions of those who can observe, first resolves of those whose instincts are large. They are seldom wrong. It is our reason which misleads us; our judgment that errs; instinct seldom, if ever. Thus it is that woman is so seldom wrong in her first resolves. When I had resided a short time in that monstrous assemblage of bricks and mortar, commonplace and sham, London, where all is sham, I said to my Cockney friends, that in London it seemed to me "to rain every other day." Some looked grave, others laughed at the idea and thought that I must mean Liverpool or Glasgow, where, thanks be to Providence! it rains every day and sometimes snows. So I tried again, and next time fancied that it was not every other day, but not much under that, And now I find, after a lapse of thirty years, that my youthful instinct and common observation were as good as modern statistics, which show that of three hundred and sixty-five days, there are in London one hundred and sixty-two on which it rains. But I must return to the semi-Catholic village, in which we halted but for an hour, to bait, that is, to refresh; and journeying onwards, our resting-place for the evening was, I think, the Murray Arms, in a suburb bearing the relation to Dumfries which Southwark does to London; that is, occupying the southern bank of the river.

It was late; but we were up early to explore the Nith from the mill-dam, adjoining the town, to the sea; and in search of many things, especially of that which has not yet been found, "the mouth of the river."

A good official, a red-tape man of great experience and authority, observed to somebody that he never knew a session pass over in the Commons House of Parliament, without there being placed before it a Salmon Fishery Bill. Whence this care for salmon?—this anxiety for the due preservation of salmon? Is salmon an essential article of food for this great nation? Who eats salmon? Why all this agitation about salmon? I will tell you. The proprietors of salmon rivers sit in both Houses; they are men of large influence; they are, or at least many of them are, the hereditary heirs of at least the properties, and of most of the privileges of the ancient Norman robbers—I was about to say or barons—almost synonymous terms—who were, by right of the sword, the heirs of similar Saxon landlords; they legislate for the nation, and especially for themselves; but the salmon rivers, as they are called, belong to them; salmon is a delicate and most excellent fish; the first of all fishes, the most prized, hence the legislation about salmon. This legislation extends to trout, that is, to the sea or salmon-trout, and will extend by and by to other trout, of which I must speak at great length anon.

We, with fishing-rods and basket, early next morning reached the banks of the Nith, so celebrated in song, duly prepared for whatever might happen. We made at once for the north side of the river, and commenced a sort of survey at and below the bridge. What first engaged our attention was a matter of which I full well knew the history; the stone steps and resting-places, invented by a most ingenious friend, to enable the salmon, in their annual migrations up the river, to surmount the powerful river wall or mill-dam constructed a short way below the town. Ingenious man! your ideas were wholly mechanical: spinning jennies, cogs and wheels, reels and levers, steam-engines, rails! Your courage and confidence in the powers of machinery were indomitable, thoroughly Saxon; subsoil ploughs, artificial drains for Nature's watercourses, canals instead of rivers; nothing seemed to please you that Nature had done. Hills you levelled, and level grounds you made hilly. Thoroughly Saxon, you could let nothing alone. Talk of going ahead! I defy the most out-and-out Kentuckian to beat you. Yet, like these men of the Far West—men of your own race, kith and kin, blood and bone—you were beaten sometimes. I have heard that you sustained a defeat in the Hebrides; somewhere about the Harris or the Lewes, whose bleak and desolate bog and peat morasses, heath-clad, rocky, barren hills, you proposed converting into grassy, verdant, well-watered plains—Devonshire meadows, irrigated and fertile! Admirable idea! But you forgot that you were in the land of the Celt. The man who is born and brought up and dies at last in poverty, misery, famine absolute, by the banks of lakes abounding in glorious trout, at the sight of which old Izaak's eyes would have sparkled; trout finer than any he ever saw, and yet the Celt on the banks of these lakes knows not even of their existence, makes no effort to take them; for him, reduced to villanage and misery by Celtic landlordism, Nature has spread out her choicest gifts in vain. But we must leave the Hebrides for a while, and return to the Nith.

The tide influences the river as high, if I rightly recollect, as this mill-dam just below the town, and which, but for it, would naturally affect it still further towards the interior of the country, or until the increasing elevation of the bed of the river renders its disturbance impossible by any tide. The tide in the Nith was beginning to ebb as we gained the opposite or northern bank. On a sunny day these banks must be beautiful —Scotland is beautiful! but how many sunny days have you? Here lies the difficulty. It is the glorious sunlight, clear, warm, and balmy, fleecy clouds, blue skies, purple heath, and verdant sward, which alone can make Scotland beautiful. Without the sunshine, all is barren, melancholy, dreary, desolate. The valley of the Nith forms no exception to this any more than the valley of the Isis, the Derwent or the Trent, the Seine or the Loire. Kaffraria itself, Nature's grand park, have I seen gloomy, cold, and desolate. The period, it is true, was but short: a day or two at most in a year. Winter is always winter, and tells even on the banks of the beauteous Keiskamma and Koonap. As we lay in our *laager* on that stormy and rainy night, awaiting daylight and fine weather to enable us to attack with success the residence and chief village of the redoubted Slambie, who, with his bold Kaffirs, was at no great distance, and ere night fell well aware of our presence, the morning came foggy, damp, and miserable. It had rained all night, and for the first time I fancied myself once more in smoky, gloomy, miserable England. But soon the glorious sun, rising in all his splendour from the eastern ocean, chased away these fogs and mists, which rested heavily on hill and plain, revealing to us the snow-clad Anatolo, projected on the azure sky, bathed in light. What a landscape was that. Nature's landscape. But I must not dwell on it here. The valley of the Nith, though infinitely marred by human hands, yet offers a beautiful landscape in its way. A tidal stream; boats, and huts, and fishermen; grassy banks, streams—gentle, it is true—and long, straight or winding reaches; a sloop at anchor; whilst not far off, but on the southern bank, rises a granite mountain of no mean height. As we journeyed along the river banks, it was easy to see that the tide had fallen considerably, leaving exposed that debatable ground, the space between high-water mark and low-water mark—a space generally understood to belong to no one, not even to the crown, but to the nation, to all. To a certain extent, it does, no doubt; but were it not for the navigation of a tidal river, and the necessity there is for suffering no interference with, or permanent obstruction of a space over which a vessel may have to pass on her way to her destined port, I am inclined to believe that this space would long since have been taken full possession of by the land proprietors. We have all heard of the love of gold; but to me the love of land seems the stronger of the two. On this neutral space, which is strictly neither dry land nor river, nor sea, at times belonging to each, and about a mile below the bridge, we overtook a party preparing to fish the river," with an apparatus so effective, so killing, so instructive, that had all the anglers in Britain— headed by my venerable senior; by the good and worthy archdeacon he also of chemical memory, together with poor Sir Charles—fished this river for centuries, they could not have arrived at equally important results.

The instruments I speak of were—

1st. A coble, or boat; 2nd. A very powerful widely-extended net, sufficient to command the river; 3rd. A couple of oars. The boats of Celtic men seldom have two oars; one having been broken a considerable time ago, and forgotten to be repaired; and I have known a party try to do without oars altogether. On the Wye, the race prefer the coracle, as they did in Caesar's time. 4th. Two men and a boy. I looked with delight at the whole party, and saw that I was about to witness that which I never hoped for—a good salmon and trout tidal river fished a distance of some miles, from an obstructing wear or dam to the Solway, or Great Sea Bay, in which the Nith, Eden, and some other rivers terminate, with a closely meshed net—an illegal neg as I had thought—yet used in open day by the tenant of the river-fishings. The mesh of the net seemed to me about three, quarters of an inch, and accordingly I expected it to do what literally I really found it did—namely, scour the river, taking everything, from a small sized minnow and herring-fry upwards, to the silvery glorious salmon.

The tenant who managed the net was a young man, practical, and quite above-board. I asked him if he would allow me to accompany the boat in its passage down the river, observe what was taken, and purchase some of the specimens; all was accorded at once: I had my choice of all the fish caught, paying for them an extremely moderate sum. Thus they fished the river for about two miles or more, shooting the net across each stream and pool by means of the boat, and hauling it ashore on the same side from which they start. Thus they fished until the rising tide forced them to desist. The sandy, barren, desolate shores of the Solway might now be seen in the distance. Sea birds began to appear; flat-fish or small flounders were now taken in the net, if my memory be correct. The appearance of herring-fry in the stream, about an inch-and-a-half in length, told us that we were in brackish water, never quite sweet, never quite salt. A sort of estuary, in fact, and just the sort of debatable ground in which a lawyer likes to found an argument; for with him it is all argument.

Now, what were the kinds of fish—the species and the genera as naturalists say, the sub-genera and the varieties, a kind of sub-species—which we caught with the silver hook? The smallest taken were, perhaps, the minnow and loch next the fry of the herring; then the parr, the celebrated, mysterious parr; the river trout, of which there seemed two kinds at least, it may be three or four distinct species; the beauteous fish in these waters called the hirling; the sea or salmon-trout; the salmon itself. Following the example of illustrious Izaak, I may as well begin with the minnow, a freshwater fish he has not failed to describe.

To the grown-up angler minnows are of no interest, saving that occasionally he would give the world, as the phrase is, to have a few fresh ones—small, sparkling, firm, just taken, plump. Finding yourself on the banks of the Whitadder or Blackadar, or Tweed, or Teviot, on a warm summer evening; the water dark and somewhat foamy, full and sweeping; soft rains have swollen the rivers and streams. And now you want some minnows; but where are they to be had? Perhaps you have brought some salted ones, and I have known such answer tolerably well. In England they have all sorts of artificial minnows, of silver and of brass, bright, burnished, like nothing that ever came from Nature's hands; and you may buy also artificial minnows tolerably well coloured, so as to resemble the real. Between the milldam of Abbey St. Bathan's and the first heavy stream opposite the Retreat, I have caught in the Whitadder, with eight salted minnows, withered and dried up, six large trout, not one of which could be readily stowed away in the basket.

I never used an artificial minnow in my life, and so have no experience of this kind of bait. Fresh-water fish, and others, show sometimes fits of stupidity, during which they will bite at almost anything; at other times, nothing can tempt them. They are highly nervous, and it is said, even mesmeric: I know the powers of electricity—of a thunder-cloud for example, suddenly appearing; this I have seen spoil instantly a noble day's sport.

But to return. A minnow is an excellent bait for trout: it is the best, for it takes all the largest. You may fish with it in the smallest streams or largest rivers, in still water or in the rapid flowing current; at all times of the year, late in autumn, early in spring. To be a perfect angler with minnow, you must have a strong arm and hand, and be at least five feet ten inches high. The minnow must be made to touch the waters as softly as a fly: it .must be made to spin or revolve dexterously, and must show life by motion, although it be dead: for trout generally will not look at a straight and dead minnow, dragged by an unskilful fisher through the waters. Fishing for trout with a minnow is the most difficult mode of angling. It requires real dexterity—that is, if you are to fish, as it were openly, on the bank. The strength of the stream is your point, near some eddy or sunken rock; a rough stream full of large stones, long since fallen into the river. Such you find in mountain passes, where the river is making its way from one valley to another. But you may fish with minnow, successfully if dexterously, in brooks and small streams, standing well back, and cautiously dropping the minnow over the bank at the top of the stream. An excellent minnow fisher, a clergyman, who fished to supply the larder, assured me that, sauntering one clear, cold, and dreary day, along the banks of the Whitadder, the river low, the east wind blowing, and hopeless of success, he merely, in sport, threw the minnow across the river, to a point where a small mountain streamlet, more like a drain, joins the main stream, never dreaming that there could be any trout there, or if there, any fish would be found insane enough to take the bait. But so it was, for four large trout came out in succession from their hiding-places, and were successively taken.

I have myself seen something like this, but nothing quite so bad, and can account for it' only by imagining that during the prevalence of the easterly winds in Britain, neither man nor fish are absolutely in their senses. Such seems to have been the opinion of that chief of wits, Voltaire: he is thought by many continental people to have rediscovered Britain and the English nation, at that period unknown to the continental nations. Wit of all wits! satirist of all satirists! dreaded by all, even Gibbon—the immortal Gibbon—was jealous of you, and tried to snarl at you: he was afraid of your "Moeurs des Nations," and I do not wonder at it. The easterly winds of Britain did not escape your notice, though they did that of ancient Izaak. Anglers do not like them, no more do trout, it would seem, nor Londoners. Nevertheless, I have had, on a Scottish river, an evening's sport whilst a strong east wind blew, which all but exceeded any I ever saw: it was in September. To this I shall return when speaking of the Whitadder. Minnow fishing, to be entirely successful in small waters, where the trout are shy, requires you to carry a small jar, filled with fresh water and a good stock of live minnows. These you use when required. When trout are shy, they must be tempted with a fresh minnow, untouched, and but that moment used. With these precautions you may take trout in the smallest rivulets; for, indeed, it is often there that the largest trout are found. But to enjoy a day's sport, seek the banks of the Whitadder, and fish that first of all trout streams from the Blackweel to the Cauldron Linn, on a July or August day, the waters full and dark, the sky cloudy, air soft. One stream may suffice. Scene of my early youth! where oft have I wandered, dreaming of the future and the what I had read of foreign lands, which I myself was destined one day to visit.

The minnows caught by the net in the Nith were like other minnows; and they are mentioned here and described here, not as being in themselves peculiar, but by indication of the smallness of the meshes of the net to warrant a belief that nothing much escaped it. I was watching the exploration of a stream I had never thought to have seen fished in this way; a stream on whose banks, some miles higher up, many ingenious experiments were made, or said to have been made, in order to ascertain what a parr is; experiments made by men uneducated, deeply prejudiced, despisers of scientific truth. I shall show, by and by, how their experiments failed. In the meantime, I should like my reader, whether angler or not, to note carefully with me what the net showed to be in the river Nith, from the mill-dam to the Solway, or nearly so, during an autumnal day. The fish caught in the net were, to the best of my recollection, minnows and small flounders; the fry of what the intelligent tacksman and my own convictions decided to be that of herring, the salmon, the salmon-trout, the hirling, the parr, river trout of two kinds,— one delicate to eat, with pink-coloured flesh; the other a coarser fish as to flavour, and strongly resembling the common trout of the Nith, taken in the river and streams above the dam, and now found in those waters in which lawyers have so often fished with great success, namely, "the waters, or rivers, or parts of rivers, into which the tide ebbs and flows." All these on our return to the inn, we examined carefully; their external appearance, their interior anatomy, the food found in their stomachs. But in the meantime, whilst watching by your banks, beauteous and melancholy Nith! the sweep of the net, examining the contents of each cast, selecting therefrom what we chose—pleasant and interesting conversation with the tacksman made the time so short, that when, by the flowing of the tide, our fishing was stopped for the day, it seemed but an hour. It was much more; and the contents of a long range of river, of an interesting character, were thus unexpectedly disclosed to me. Here 1 could observe Nature as she acted, untrammelled by human hands, human experiments. It was an hour I look back to with delight: for to discover the unknown, a new truth in science, a new relation of observed phenomena, has ever afforded me the most intense pleasure.

The opinion of the tacksman amounted to this, that minnows are simply minnows, and do not grow into any other kind of fish: that parrs are parrs, hirling simply hirling, and that salmon-trout and salmon are fishes perfectly distinct. But of the trout found in the river, of two kinds, as already remarked, he had a theory, which was this: -

At the distance of a mile or two from the south-western bank of the river, where we then stood, pleasantly discussing the point, there is a small lake, in which are found the so-much-prized pink-coloured lake trout—that is, trout with the muscles or flesh tinged like salmon. Sometimes, no doubt, he remarked, some of these trout make their way into the Nith, by the small streams through which are discharged the surplus waters of the lake, and having once got into the river, they cannot return to the lake, by reason of the falls in the stream. This was his theory. I doubt its correctness.

In the lower part of the Tyne (see Chapter II), from the bridge to Tyningham Sands, in East Lothian, I had already found a pink-coloured red-spotted trout, of exquisite flavour— habits and food peculiar; and this same trout, as appeared to me, exists also in the tidal portion of the Nith. Of this peculiar kind of fish I have already said enough. I have elsewhere called it the Estuary Trout, meaning by this name simply to express a fact that it is taken only in those parts of rivers into which the tide ebbs and flows. Besides, lake trout have dark spots, whilst the trout I speak of had red spots, like those of the estuary of the Tyne. I state this latter fact from memory, without a reference to my notes, but I believe it will be found correct.

CHAPTER VIII

THE ANNAN; LOCHMABEN, CASTLE OE ROBERT DE VENGIS

The town of Annan is some three or four hours' walk from Dumfries. The angler may travel it as he thinks fit. Bub when arrived at Annan he is not on angling ground, properly speaking; and I bring him here merely to have a gossip with him about the Solway and its stake-net fishings. It is near Annan Foot that the dangerous Solway is crossed at the ebb of tide. Should you purpose doing so on foot, or on horseback, be sure to have a guide with you, lest the terrible "bore" of the Solway overtake you in your course. Whilst examining the stake-nets at the mouth of the Solway, I became aware how dangerous it is for a stranger to wander heedlessly upon the banks when abandoned by the tide. The flood returns, rushing up the deep excavations, which you do not observe when the bed of the Frith is dry, but which become impassable as the tide flows. We escaped climbing along a stake-net, and had a sharp run for it.

There is no angling that I know of about here. Large salmon and enormous bull trout are said to ascend the Annan in autumn and early in winter. They are fished by poachers, and salted down for winter food. I should not like to partake of such food. By the condiments of salt and vinegar, they are probably rendered safe, to a certain extent. I do not like to eat. anything found dead in the fields, nor would I touch a salmon or sea trout found dead by the river side. The fish of which I speak are not found dead, it is true, but in a condition wholly unfit as food for man.

We had examined the stake-nets extending from Annan Foot, westward towards the Frith, and had gone eastward from Annan Foot towards the Eden, to prosecute an inquiry into the history of net-fishing for salmon. It was autumn, but a cold north-easterly wind swept the valley of the Solway. As we travelled onwards on foot by the slimy disagreeable banks, my companion suddenly became ill; he could just walk. I felt inconceivably and suddenly exhausted; but in the sight of one worse than myself, I always recover so much strength, at least as to be able to assist. We turned our steps towards Annan, sitting down often by the roadside to rest, although the distance we had walked that morning was really nothing to us. As we neared the town of Annan, where horse and gig, and dinner awaited us, I looked westward, and beheld a singular phenomenon. Over the locality where I knew Dumfries stood, there shot, from earth to heaven, a dark mist. I could not call it a cloud, it was of considerable breadth, it resembled nothing I had ever seen, and the only think I could compare it to was a vast column of living insects on the wing, hovering over Dumfries, and not unlike one of Turner's latest productions, when despising all colour and form he attempted something original. But that it was a cloud of insects was probably a delusion, or optical deception at least, not impossible, but very doubtful. I wish that the author of the "Historic Doubts" respecting the reign of Napoleon Buonaparte had distinctly perceived, which apparently he could not do, the difference between the possible and impossible, the defeat of great armies by one man, and the cutting through a whetstone with a razor by another. But to return to the mist over Dumfries. As I gazed until I felt a mysterious awe, and said to my friend that I liked not its appearance whatever it might forebode, we were due east of that mist; so acting on instinct, as I prefer doing when permitted, the horse was ordered, and, in an hour, we were on our road to Lochmaben.

On ascending the high grounds, by which we cleared the valley of the Solway, my friend got better, long before we reached the lovely banks of the Castle Loch of Lochmaben; and by next morning, when, rod in hand, and basket ready, we prepared to fish the Annan, the whole circumstance was forgotten.

On returning from the river-side to our inn, we learned what startled us: the Angel of Death had visited Dumfries the evening before; that is, on the evening following the afternoon on which I had seen from Annan the fatal cloud hovering over that town. Was this the cause? What connexion had this mist with the Asiatic pestilence, which swept Dumfries on that fatal night? I answer not, leaving all to judge for themselves. Of the real nature of this dreadful pestilence nothing is known, nor of any other pestilence. During its visitation to Britain, I had several opportunities of verifying the remark of Thucydides, whilst speaking of the plague at Athens. "The physicians at first, could administer no relief, through utter ignorance; nay, they died the faster the closer their attendance on the sick; and all human art—first and last—was totally unavailing."

Behold us now at Lochmaben, and close to the Annan and the AE, both good trouting streams; but above all, as regards scenery, in the neighbourhood of that beautiful lake, the Castle Loch of Lochmaben; and on its shady banks the ruined Castle of "the Brus." Here, if we can trust history, lived one of the great Norman robbers, called Robert de Brus. He had other castles besides this one, for the original seat of the family was Guisborough, in Yorkshire; the Scotch estates came, I think, by marriage. The castle has a still stronger interest than even this, though Bannockburn will live long in story; this castle was one of the residences of Marie Stuart, queen of Scotland. The lake, which at one time had surrounded the castle by means of an artificial moat, contains fish of various kinds, but not many trout. Pike abound, but chief and foremost is the vengis or vendiss, thought to have been transplanted to this lake by the early monks. Of this curious and beautiful fish, a number of idle stories were told, until the rubbish was cleared away by myself; the most curious part of its history was, that it could not be tempted by any bait. Now this was true, and the cause thereof was demonstrated for the first time by myself. The vendiss live on minute microscopic entomostraca, a kind of shellfish, declining all other food.

Before I describe the vengis or vendiss, let me say a few words about angling in the Annan. It is not a particularly good river for this purpose, being much poached and scourged by the idle and profligate of the village. But it contains trout and parr, sea trout and hirling, salmon and bull trout in their season; besides pike and bream, and other coarse fish. The country around is primitive, and many originals live on its banks, and around the lakes of Lochmaben. The vendiss, shorn of its mystery, is still fished at a particular time of the year with nets, and ate in season—a kind of whitebait dinner for some old-fashioned people. It brings them together — suspends for an hour or two the little animosities which all farmers and small lairds have to their next neighbours—and benefits the inns. When other topics fail, they talk of Johnny Armstrong and the Border robbers. Abhorring clubs and whitebait dinners, I always avoided these vendiss clubs, but I have often eaten the vendiss when just from the lake. It is a moderately good fish to eat, but not to be compared to the Loch Leven trout. The professed naturalist arranges the vendiss with the family of the Corrigoni, a hard word to pronounce. Vendiss is better and softer, so is vengis, of whose root we know nothing. A fish of the same sort, but specifically different, is abundant enough in Loch Lomond. They occur also, though not of the same species, in Wales; in North America the natural family abounds.

CHAPTER IX

OF FISH CALLED PARR, BRANDLIN, FINGERLING, ETC.

This singular fish, whose natural history is still so mysterious, is found only in rivers frequented by salmon; I was about to add, or by salmon-trout; but of this I am not quite sure. In the small stream which drains the area of that valley in Cleveland which once claimed for a resident proprietor the celebrated Robert de Brus—in this stream, which passes close to the village of Guisborough, abundance of sea trout of the largest size frequent at the "due season of the year," but no parr are ever found; but common trout reside permanently in the stream; and this leads me to the conclusion: 1st, that as sea trout may frequent streams in which the parr is not to be found, the common parr cannot then belong to the sea trout; and 2ndly, were the parr a hybrid between the sea trout and the common river trout frequenting these streams, we should again have had the parr.

Thus we endeavour to narrow the curious and obscure question of the origin of the parr, the most abundant of all our fresh-water fishes of the trout kind; of all, the least understood.

I revert to my first statement. Parr are found only in rivers frequented by salmon, but not in all rivers frequented by the king of fishes. Parr are not found in the Kale, in Roxburghshire, nor in the Tyne, in Haddingtonshire. This I know has been denied, but I am too sure of my facts to doubt them.

My esteemed friend, Mr. Young, of Invershin, informs me by letter, that parr are found in certain streams into which neither salmon nor salmon trout ever penetrated. Notwithstanding so high authority—the best, I believe—I must venture still to doubt. The parr he means must be the parr-trout, which I have often seen mistaken for parr by good and experienced anglers. It seems to me that Nature herself has settled this part of the question by an experiment she has made on a great scale; the river Clyde is the seat of the experiment. Below the falls of Stone Byres, parr abound in incredible numbers, at least in autumn; above the falls trace the river to its source, you never will take a single parr. It is the same, I believe, everywhere else; interrupt the course of the salmon, and with it the parr disappears.

The theories offered to explain the natural history of the parr are the necessary results of our ignorance of the habits of the parr; were these known, no theory need be offered. In the absence of a knowledge of the facts, it has been conjectured: 1st, that the parr is simply the young of the salmon and of the salmon trout. But the streams of Guisborough disprove this idea as regards the salmon-trout, and so there need no more be said about it.

That the parr is the young of the true salmon, is the oldest of all the theories. On the Annan, the fishermen universally entertain this idea: it had prevailed for at least a hundred years. They did not seem to be aware that any other theory had ever been proposed. Mr. Hogg, the Ettrick Shepherd, as he was called, made experiments to prove the theory, which by many were deemed satisfactory.

As early, however, as 1794, Mr. Hutchinson, of Carlisle, objecting to this view, endeavoured to prove the parr to be a species of fish distinct from all others. He failed to convince anyone; and for this simple reason: he never could find a female parr with the roe developed; that is, a female parr, preparing to deposit those ova on which must depend the perpetuity of the race. Without this proof, the natural history of the parr cannot be said to exist.

Mr. Hutchinson was the first to observe (1794), without comprehending the meaning of what the transcendental anatomy can alone explain, that if from off the sides of a true salmon fry, or smolt, the silvery scales be carefully scraped, the young fish will show all the parr markings concealed by these scales;" and besides these so-called parr-spots or bars, there will then appear the dark-coloured spots peculiar to some trout, and the red-coloured spots peculiar to others. From these observations, implying much quickness of observation, Mr. Hutchinson drew at least no false conclusions; but this was afterwards done; and the Keith Medal was bestowed by the

Royal Society of Edinburgh, on the writer of a memoir in which
we find "the generic characters of the embryo salmon" mistaken
for specific; the parr declared to be a salmon, because it has
some of the characters of the salmon smolt; and the salmon
declared to be in its younger days a parr, because, in its
development from the egg to the smolt, it displays, with all
other animals, those embryo forms connecting it not merely
with the natural family of the salmonidæ, but with the
zoological, and, more especially, the ichthyological world, past,
present, and to come.

We have seen that the objection taken by M. Valenciennes to
the theory I now speak of, rested mainly on the dentition of the
parr. He thinks that natural history characters can with propriety
be taken only from the adult individual of each species. But this
just remark does not at all inform us what the fish we call parr
and the French *tacon* is. If the parr and *tacon* be distinct species
of trout, the female with fully developed roe ought to exist.
Now this has not been shown. It has, indeed, been stated, that a
female parr with the roe well developed has been seen, though
very rarely. Seeing the extreme rarity of such a phenomenon, it
would have been desirable to have preserved the specimen,
submitting it to scientific men. A female mule has been known
to produce a colt; it is just possible; but the phenomenon is
almost as rare as "birds with four legs, and griffins." But were it
even true, it would not prove the parr to be a salmon.

The question seems to be a narrow one, but, in fact, it is not
so. What are the facts? What the conjectures? What the
difficulties? At a certain time of the year, we find universally, in
rivers frequented by salmon and sea trout, but in none else, a
little silvery fish, gregarious, in vast numbers, which nobody
doubts being a young salmon. This is in the end of April and
early in May; no such fish are to be found in any river at any
other time of the year. Of these young salmon, I have examined
hundreds, and have found no milt nor roe in the slightest degree
altered, or showing any appearance that it had ever been so;
these organs were constantly at their minimum. I wish the
reader particularly to note this. These young salmon leave in a

body for the ocean, and so disappear. Some of them return, we are assured by the experimentalists, in a few weeks, grown into large grilses of several pounds, weight. Now, I think it most probable, that all do not return so early and so well grown, but that some may ascend the rivers in August and September, not more than half-a-pound weight: whilst others which had descended very early, so soon perhaps as February, may come up early in March; but this is mere conjecture, and I prefer viewing these anomalous fishes as the young of the hirling. To return to facts.

After the fry, as salmon smolts have left the rivers in May, there remain in the main stream and its tributaries innumerable fish of a doubtful character called parr. They may be caught with the ordinary bait for trout in every stream and pool— from the sources, for example, of the Tweed to its junction with the sea; they were taken with the net in the tidal part of the Nith, in my presence, and in numbers, in August and September; I have caught them in the rivers at all times of the year; they vary in size from two and a-half or two inches to six or seven, and their growth seems independent of any season. But that which is most remarkable, and is without an example in zoology, is, that early in summer, and from this time to February and March, many of the males of these dubious fishes have the milt exceedingly developed; the roe in the female remaining uniformly and without any exception at its minimum. By supposing that these dubious fish with embryonic markings are young salmon, not yet grown into smolts, or, in other terms, which have not as yet laid aside their embryonic colouring and characteristics, we simply add other enigmas to those already existing. For how comes it, that being fully as large as the smolt, they have not left with it? How comes it, that whilst still so young (not being even as yet smolts), the male should have the milt enormously developed, not only whilst in this state, that is, before he has even become a smolt, but long before the adult salmon itself? For the male parr has the milt fully developed quite as frequently in July and August as in November and December. The fact is, that these facts, for they are such, as I shall presently prove, not merely upset the existing theories, but show that the question of the parr is one involving the highest questions in animal physiology, and explicable, in all probability, only by an appeal to the laws regulating hybridism and transcendentalism in animal life.

It has been said that parrs have been placed in ponds, and have grown into salmon. That they may grow into fish strongly resembling salmon, I am not disposed to doubt, although I do not feel quite sure that the experiment has ever been fairly made; but this does not prove them to be true salmon. The mule grows up to something strongly resembling a horse. The fish grown from parr is found to be prolific for at least one generation, which could not be were it a hybrid, or the parr from which it grew, a hybrid. Now those who argue thus, take for granted that the laws of hybridity, in all animals, correspond strictly with what happens in the horse and ass. I am sure that no educated man will expect me to argue with persons who hold such views.

Lastly, it is well known, that although in the female parr, at no time is the roe developed, yet in the male at certain, or rather, as I shall show, at uncertain periods of the year, the milt suddenly increases to a size disproportionate to the fish. With the milt of this fish, some five or six inches in length, the eggs of the true full-grown salmon have been artificially fecundated; the, product being true salmon.

In such experiments I see nothing remarkable. They do not prove the male parr to be a salmon. On the contrary, the growth of the milt in the parr is an unnatural and abnormal phenomenon, proving directly the contrary, proving it not to be the true salmon. All the world knows that towards the end of April, and beginning of May, the salmon smolt, varying from five to six inches in length, often larger than any parr, abounds in salmon rivers; but no one ever saw the milt or roe developed in these smolts. How comes it, then, that in the parr, if a salmon, the milt should be developed a year before it becomes a smolt? It is singular enough that in parr with the milt thus developed, we do not find that the individual has deteriorated in quality as is the case in other fish similarly situated. True, it may be said that this is not the period for the growth of the milt; but I shall show presently that this remark does not apply to the parr, which shows the milt developed at seasons of the year in which no salmon is ever found with these organs progressing towards a fecundating condition.

The phenomenon then is an abnormal and irregular one, proving the parr to belong to no peculiar species of fish, but a hybrid of several sorts; that the word parr is, in fact, a generic term for the young of several species of the salmonidæ, of which some are regular and constant, others irregular and hybrid.

FURTHER CONTRIBUTIONS TO THE NATURAL HISTORY OF THE PARR.

Is it worth while writing the history of an animal which perhaps exists not as a distinct species? In this case, I think it is. Many facts still remain wholly unexplained in the history of the parr; I shall here state those which have come within my own knowledge.

The parr, under a variety of names, is found in most of the rivers of Great Britain, Ireland, and perhaps also of France and Germany, frequented by salmon. It seldom exceeds nine inches in length. The parr-trout, and the young of salmon, and of sea trout, are often mistaken for the parr.

In its dentition it resembles the trout, having maxillary, intermaxillary, mandibular, lingual, palatine, and vomerine teeth. These last are in two interrupted or alternating rows, as in the trout; they are scarcely so numerous, and occasionally they show a disposition to carry transverse teeth on the forepart (chevron) of the vomer, which no true trout does. In this, and in its silvery scales and bluish tinge, it shows its partly salmon parentage.

In the parr the spleen is oval and small, triangular in the trout of the same size, and somewhat larger: it is triangular also in the salmon and sea trout.

Parr may be taken during every month of the year in the tributaries and streams which form the sources of the Tweed. They are found throughout the year in the Annan and its feeders. If the view I take of the smolt or salmon-fry be correct, namely, that on quitting the gravel they do not remain longer than from three to five weeks in the fresh-water rivers, then the parr cannot be the same as that fry, since they are found at all times of the year in the rivers and streams. But if incorrect, the fry might be found in the rivers, imperfectly developed, and resembling parr and trout in their habits and external and internal characters. Let us now consider this first point: let us suppose that young salmon may really remain in the rivers, in one form or another, from about the beginning of April of one year to the beginning of May of the year following, should we expect to find, in any pure species of fish, a phenomenon so extraordinary as the development of the milt, in a great majority of cases, at times of the year when the fully grown fish shows no such state, the roe of the female in the meantime remaining uniformly at its minimum?

If we admit the parr to be a true salmon, all these contradictory laws must be applied to him: here are the proofs:

I. Examine, as I have done, hundreds and hundreds of the true salmon smolt, whilst descending the rivers, sparkling with their silvery scales, and obviously "salmon in miniature," towards the ocean; and the roe and the milt will constantly be found at their *minimum*; that is, mere threads. And yet, after all these have left the river for the ocean, we almost immediately find the parr with the milt or male organs in the highest state of development. If these were smolts not yet sufficiently grown, how comes it that their brothers of a year older growth, as is said, have left the river with the milt at its minimum, leaving behind them their younger brothers with the same organ at its maximum?

It is worthy, moreover, of observation, as showing the irregularity of the phenomena as respects the parr, that even in December all male parr have not the milt developed, but only a certain number.

1st. On the 30th July, 1832, sic parr were caught with the artificial fly, at Romano Bridge, on the Lyne, a tributary of the Tweed. They were of the usual size, averaging probably five inches. All were males, with the milts large, and two and a quarter inches in length. Do we find salmon usually with the milt large in July?

2nd. At the Crook (on Tweed side), on the 31st of July, that is, next day, of ten fish taken with the artificial fly, sic were parrs; they were much in the same state as the above.

3rd. Of thirteen parrs caught on the 3rd of September, in the Tweed, between Bield Bridge and Palnoudie, two only were females; the rest were males. Some were eight and a-half inches long, others only four or five. In the larger the milts were enormously developed. This was on the 3rd September, so that if they were salmon they had the advantage of unheard-of precocity, being advanced by many months before the full-grown salmon.

I had some parr, twenty-four in all, caught for me in the AE, a tributary of the Annan. This was on the 13th December. Of these, fourteen were female parr; they were all caught with a small red worm. The average length of these parr was five and a-half inches; the smallest three inches. The roe in all, without any exception, was at its minimum.

Of the other ten males, caught on the same day, in the same place, some had the milt large and vascular, but not so much so as I have seen in July and August.

In four of these ten the milt was at its minimum, having undergone no changes.

For the establishment and identification of distinct species, it may freely be admitted, that the anatomical method is at once the safest and the best; and, when combined with the external characters of the grown individual, leaves nothing to be desired. But the case is somewhat different, and the method less valuable in a practical sense, when applied to the young, and still more so to the hybrid, which I consider the parr to be.

The dentition, for example, seems to be the same in the parr, smolt, and trout. I use the word seems, for I am not aware of any minute anatomical inquiries having been made on this point by others, and I cannot find, amongst the mass of notes before me, the memoranda made at various times by my brother and myself. The teeth of the salmonidæ, as well as of most fishes, are of uniform character, and present no such distinctions as molar, incisor, and canine, by which we are enabled so clearly and easily to note the various species of mammals. But they are carried on a greater number of bones, and from this specific characters may be deduced. In the having maxillary, intermaxillary, mandibular, palatine, and vomerine teeth, all the salmonidæ agree; but they differ when adult in respect of the number and arrangement of the vomerine.

In the common trout, the vomerine teeth are abundant (20) are arranged in two interrupted rows, with the points turned outwards, neither being precisely mesial. Many of the finest of this species of trout have no transverse vomerine teeth, or, at least, no row entitled to that name; but others have: in certain sea trout, at least, the vomerine system of teeth consists in a few apparently mesial teeth, arranged in a single row, and a transverse row on the chevron, whilst in the true salmon the mesial teeth are still fewer, or absent, and the transverse row still more distinct. .

But circumstances necessarily render the characteristics of dentition inapplicable in the case of the parr. For, 1st., it seems all but certain that the smolt and parr have a dentition neither resembling the adult trout nor adult salmon, but uniting the features of both: a type of itself. 2nd. The dentition is a characteristic not altogether to be depended on, not from any error in itself, but from the want of extended research.

Anxious to investigate the subject of the dentition of the parr and of the smolt, I wrote to my friend, Mr. Young, of Invershin, to furnish me with a few. The results will be given below.

II. For obvious reasons, the characteristics of species derived from the strength of the head and jaws, of the respiratory apparatus, or gills and gill-covers, and of the locomotive organs, the fins, are much less distinct, much less to be depended on, in the young and imperfectly developed animal than in the adult. In this direction, therefore, I have not sought for any. The same remark applies to the system of colouration of the surface, which, in the adult, when combined with other natural history characters, and backed by the anatomical history of the animal, furnishes valuable discriminations of species, but in the young or imperfectly grown individuals is of little real value.

III. The number of spines composing the fins seems to me a means of assisting in the determination of species. Comparing, then, the undoubted parr and smolt, of the same size, taken from the same river, but not at the same time, the result was as follows:

		Perfect.	Imperfect.		Perfect.	Imperfect.
Pectoral fin	Parr	11	3	Smolt	13	
Ventral fin	"	8	2	"	9	
Caudal fin	"	17	9	"	19	12
Dorsal fin	"	11	4	"	10	12
Anal fin	"	8	3	"	10	3

By imperfect ray or spine is meant merely those scarcely annulated rays which do not bifurcate, and do not reach the margin of the fin. The others bifurcate. The memorandum giving the above details adds other particulars. The specimen was a male, and the spleen measured $1\frac{1}{8}$ by $\frac{3}{8}$. I think that this remark has a reference to the parr. The sex of the smolt is not mentioned. The length of the parr was $7\frac{2}{8}$ inches; girth, $4\frac{1}{8}$; breadth, $1\frac{5}{8}$. It was caught in the Tweed on the 1st June. The stomach was gorged with the food of the common trout.

Parr will occasionally disappear for years from a river. In July, 1832, of twenty-two dozen of trout taken in one day from the Whitwater, there was not a parr. They had some years before abounded.

The term parr, then, is a generic term, applicable to several kinds of fish. The young of the sea trout, for example, like that of the salmon when it first leaves the gravel, and until it undergoes its metamorphosis as to colouration of the surface, resembles, no doubt, like the smolt or young salmon, the fish called parr. Its growth I know to be rapid. In a few weeks it loses its parr markings, and other embryonic characters, and makes for the sea.

This sufficiently curious fact, namely, that the young of the sea trout, in the smolt state, preparing to descend to the sea, resemble strictly the smolt of the true salmon, shows the caution required in making observations on the imperfectly developed animal, their peculiar colouration of numerous dark spots and specific dentition not appearing until they have resided for some time in the ocean.

An ingenious person and pleasant author has suggested some theories respecting the nature of the parr, and the generation of the salmon (subjects intimately connected with each other), which merit a passing notice.

He suggests that the parr is simply a young salmon; that it remains a year in the river after leaving the gravel, or, in other words, adopts the views, in this last point, of Young, of Invershin:—that on assuming the silvery dress it migrates towards the sea with the spawning fish of that year, and that this is the reason why no parr are caught in Teviot and Tweed during the months of April and May, they having all assumed the smolt colouring. But as the parr, meaning young salmon of the present year, begin to grow, they naturally reappear in the rivers in June, July, &c.; continuing to grow until next spring, when they also leave as smolts. To meet other difficulties, Mr. S. conjectures—for all is conjecture here—that it is when the young are in the parr form that the fecundating act takes place; the roe of the female parr being impregnated by the male when the ova are at their minimum of development, the milt of the parr being then at its maximum; and that the presence of the male full-grown salmon, at the moment the crown female deposits the ova in the spawning trough, is an accidental "circumstance, and not at all essential to secure the forthcoming brood of smolts."

It is scarcely necessary to add that these ingenious views are based neither on experiment nor observation. They seem merely like discoveries in Egyptian hieroglyphics, to solve one enigma by creating a dozen new ones, still more perplexing to chronologists.

I have already remarked that parr seem to desert some rivers, for a time at least, from causes as yet unknown. Thus, in July, of twenty-two dozen trout caught in the Whitwater near Millknow, there was not a single parr. On the other hand, in some rivers they are most abundant nearly at all times. In August, 1832, four hours' very careful fishing with fly and worm produced nothing but forty-three parrs; twenty-four males, and nineteen females. The parr has a layer of fat along the tract of the intestine, which is not present in the trout or salmon. They are more tenacious of life than the smolt, and stiffen readily in the basket. The spleen is oval and small in the parr; triangular in the trout and salmon.

On the 29th May, in the Eddlestone, about a mile from the Tweed, of twenty-eight fish caught with the fly, ten were parr. There were no smolts to be seen, although ten days before the stream was full of them, all nearly of a length, i.e., about four inches. On the 1st June, that is three days afterwards, parr were taken in the Tweed measuring inches, their brethren of our inches having in the meantime become smolts, and fled to the ocean. I venture to call Mr. Stoddart's attention to these facts. Mr. Stoddart is, I understand, a poet.

The distinction of perfect and imperfect rays or spines is based on this: by perfect is meant a spine which has one root, but which in a short time divides into two, almost in the manner of a feather; these alternately form the terminating margin of the fin. Whereas, the spines I have called imperfect are single throughout, scarcely annulated, and do not reach the terminating margin of the fin.

I had some parr fished for in the AE, a tributary of the Annan, on the 13th December; fourteen female parr were caught with a small red worm. The average length of these parr was five and a-half inches; the smallest three inches. The roe in all, without exception, in the state it is usually found in the parr; that is, in no way developed.

There were ten males caught at the same time; some of the milts were large and vascular, but not so much so as those seen there in August. In four of these males the milt was not developed. Upon the whole, these parr in December are in much the same condition in this respect as in August.

Some observations show a disproportion of males to females, the former being the more numerous. Of thirteen caught on the 3rd September in the Tweed, between Bield Bridge and Palnoudie, two only were females, the rest males; some were eight and a-half inches long, others only four or five. In the largest the milts were enormously developed. This was on the 3rd September.

After all the true salmon-fry have left the river for the ocean, the parrs abound, no matter which be the season of the year. Thus I found them in the Lyne (a branch of the Tweed), at Romano Bridge, on the 30th July. Of six caught, all were males, with milts two and a-quarter inches long. At the Crook, on the 31st, often fish caught, six were parrs. In August, in the Annan, near Lochmaben, nothing was taken with the fly but parrs. Nevertheless the fishermen of the district were all of opinion that these parrs were merely young salmon.

It is worthy of observation that no direct experiments have ever been made proving the parr to be a salmon. These would require to be made with great care, and frequently repeated; for the accidental or occasional growth of a male or female parr to a salmon size, no more proves the parr to be a true salmon than a similar occurrence taking place in the mule would prove that animal to be a horse.

I have notes of thirteen parr caught in the Tweed, between the Bield and Palnoudie, and examined on the 3rd September; of these only two were female in the usual state as to the roe of the males, some had the milt enormously developed. They varied in length from four to eight and a-half inches. They were the largest parr I had ever seen.

Parr may be found rivers they frequent, from near their sources to the junction with the sea. Throughout the whole range they uniformly take the same food, that is, the food of the common trout.

I have it recorded amongst my notes that parr, about two and a-half inches long, are very numerous in March in the Annan, as far up as Hallheaths. Many of these are probably young salmon, mistaken for parrs.

During the course of last summer, I received from my friend, Mr. Young, of Invershin, a present of five small fishes, four of which he considered to be smolts, arid one a parr. On examining these with some care, I found that in some-the caeca were in two rows; in others, in three; about fifty-two in all. The vomerine teeth presented a double interrupted mesial row (as in the trout), varying from sixteen to twenty-four. In some, the transverse teeth on the chevron were distinct; but in others this could not be determined: or, at all events, the transverse row present did not extend beyond the range of the mesial rows. In the specimen which Mr. Young considers to be a parr, I found the vomerine teeth as follows:

Mesial in a double row and alternating, as in trout $8 - 8 == 16$
Anteriorly on the chevron or transverse teeth 4

Audi alteram partem; for this reason I subjoin a letter addressed to a kind friend—one, if I recollect right, of my former students; also one from my esteemed friend of Invershin:

"My dear John,—l have to acknowledge the receipt of your letter, and would have answered the same ere this had not my shooting excursions interfered more or less. However, regarding the parr and salmon, I have studied the subject much, and indeed have assisted Mr. Gillom with his experiments, closely, ever since 1838, and neither of us entertain the slightest doubt but that the parr becomes salmon the third year after being spawned.

"We conduct our experiments in the following manner:—A large tank is formed close on the bank of the Dee, through which part of that water has a free ingress and egress; and the tank is so constructed by machinery and wire netting at each end, that when the Dee rises the water in the tank rises also, and vice versa. Into this tank we put the fry, at the same time knowing it to be the salmon-fry by observing the old salmon deposit their spawn, which we can do at any time during the spawning season. The young fry, when put into the tank, are

about half an inch long, and have at that time the pea attached to their belly. The first year they do not assume much of the parr, but the second year they are decidedly so, by hundreds of comparisons with parr taken out of the Dee, and the third year they become what we call the young salmon-fry, and from four to five inches long, and quite change their colour from the parr to a silvery one; at this stage they go down to the salt water. Were we to confine them longer than the third year, by many experiments, they fall very much off. Another proof of the parr being the young salmon is, that no man ever saw a parr higher up a river than where a salmon
can go.

"Gillom tells me his first experiments were in 1835-6. In that year he put fry into an inland lake; they did very well until the third year, and then fell off, and eventually perished. He also tells me that he would not believe the parr to be young salmon until he proved it by his own experiments.

"Now I doubt much if you can make out this hurried scrawl; but if you can I hope it will tend to throw some light on the subject; if so, let me hear from you.

"Your family are well. I had the pleasure to sup in company with your father last evening. My wife joins me in kind regards to you, and believe me,

"Yours sincerely,

" A. HANNAY.

"Kirkcudbright, 18th Nov. 1841."

"Invershin, Bonar Bridge, Aug. 9th, 1852.

"My dear sir,—l duly received your favour of the 3rd instant, and will be always happy to hear from you. You are right with regard to the time the salmon-fry remain river after rising from the spawning bed. They remain twelve months, and not two years, as your Edinburgh section of naturalists tried to cram down our throats but that theory has now exploded, and the Keith medal ought to be bestowed on some more correct investigator.

"But observe, that the whale smolts do not go down with the early spring floods; the part of them then twelve months old go down as the floods happen, but there are many of them from eight to twelve months old that go down in the course of the summer, and as soon as they arrive at the age of emigration. To explain the theory better, I may mention that we have salmon spawning in the rivers at all times from the middle of September to the middle of the following March; some few may be earlier and later than these periods, but we see them at all times within that space; the seed deposited during that time remains among the gravel for the space of from 100 to 140 days, according to the temperature of the water, and, at all events, we have the seeds hatching and rising from the beds at all times during six months, and of course must have the smolts going down at all times during six months, and grilses returning at all times during six months. But the great throng of spawning is from the middle of November to the middle of December, therefore the great majority of the fry are, according to the temperature, a year old in April and May, which clearly accounts for the great majority of smolts going down in these months; from the time the smolts go down, until they return grilses, is two months; sometimes in the latter half of June, and at, other times July is the great throng of the grilses, that being exactly two months from the time the great throng of the smolts go down. The spawning begins about the middle of September, with a few pairs; they get on more and more up to the middle of November, when the great number spawn up to the middle of December, when they then fall off in numbers nearly in proportion to the increase, until the middle of March, which fully accounts for the time, and numbers of smolts going down during six months every year. It may be that they spawn and go down throughout a longer period than that, but the above we see yearly, in the spawning, smolts going down and grilses returning.

"The fry, from the age of two months (that is the time they are fully formed with fins, complete) to the age of ten months, have transverse bars, or, as they are sometimes called, finger marks, very much resembling the cross-bars on a small fullgrown fish, called the parr; and for many years the fry and the parr were confounded with one another. The greatest distinguishing mark between the two is, that the parr has fins in proportion to the fish, while the salmon-fry have fins uncommonly large for the size of the fish. The parr is to be found in salmon rivers, and also in rivers where salmon have no access. They were to be seen in hundreds in the rivers that run into and feed Lochshin, previous to the time that we planted these rivers with salmon, and until we did that there was never a salmon seen in these rivers, but now they go there yearly, and the salmon-fry and parr are both to be seen in the rivers; there is now only the little river Grudy that runs into the river Shin, where salmon have never passed a fall on that river, and where parr are yet above that fall. At some time, when the river gets low, I will get a few for you, as I am also to do for Mr. Yarrel, but am sure you can easily get them in any English river with a small fly, as you are perfectly acquainted with them, when I hope you will write something on the subject.

"I have not been in any correspondence with the Royal Society for a long time. You are aware that they expressed the two year old opinion, and that I have reduced that system to nothing, therefore such clever men do not like to be refuted, but it would be a public benefit were you to bring the subject before some naturalists there. You will see a full set of artificial bred salmon, that I sent to the Ashmolean Society, Oxford, which will enable you to see the thing more clearly.

I remain, ever yours truly, A. YOUNG. R. KNOX, Esq., M.D."

At page 63 of my MS. Journal, I find that, at my request, my esteemed friend, Mr. Harkness, of Lochmaben, fished the river AE for me with bait (a small red worm), and the Castle Loch with a net, sending me the products. From the AE were taken

fourteen female parr and ten male ditto, also one parr-trout
eleven inches long. The longest parr was seven inches, the
smallest three, the average five-and-a-half. In the female parr
the ova were distinct, but quite unaltered; in some of the male,
the milts were of considerable size, in others not developed.
Upon the whole, the parr were much in the condition I had
found them in the Tweed, in August and September. The
stomachs of these parr were full of insects. The river and lake
were fished for me in December.

PART II

THE TWEED AND ITS TRIBUTARIES.

"The groves of sweet myrtles let foreign lands reckon, Where bright
beaming summers exalt the perfume:
Far dearer to me yon lone glen of Greenbrecken,
With the burn stealing under the long yellow broom."

INTRODUCTION

Scotland is essentially a mountainous and a hilly country.
Wild and desolate mountain ranges, clothed with heath, but
devoid of trees, occupy the greater part even of the south of
Scotland. The sources of the Clyde, the Annan, and the
Tweed, and of their tributaries, point out the more elevated
parts of this region, extending from west to east, from
Earleston's Hill to Cockburn's Path; a vast circuit of many
miles, including the sources of Tweed's northern tributaries.
On the south, Tweed, the prince of all angling rivers, drains
the northern slopes of the Cheviots, receiving from these
slopes many noble angling streams.

I shall speak of those on the northern side first, and describe
the tributaries before discoursing the angling qualities of the
main stream itself, to which indeed I shall merely allude. At or
near the embouchures of the smaller streams which feed it,
each river may be said to have its own angling station; that is,
the point from which it may be most conveniently fished; and
in this respect many of the streams may be further subdivided
into upper and lower waters, generally sufficiently distinct.
These localities or head-quarters of the angler are, for the
Gala, Torsonse and Noble House; for the Leader, the Inn of
Soutra; Leader and Leader Foot; for the Blackadder, Dunse
and Greenlaw; for the Whitadder (Upper Waters), The
Cottage, six miles from Dunse; Edron and Allan Bank or
Chirnside are the stations whence may be most conveniently
fished the lower waters of the same river. For Talla and
Tweed, the Crook and Beild offer favourite shelter and
resting-places for the angler, where, reposing for the evening,

he may enjoy from the windows of his own inn a sight of Tweed's crystal stream. At Peebles, the angler may fish the Lyne, and Tweed, and Manor Waters; the Eddlestone is also close at hand; at Inverleithen he commands the Tweed itself, the Leithen, and many other excellent trouting streams; lower down is the Inn of Clovenford, a good headquarters for this part of the Tweed. Even Galashiels and Selkirk are still within reach of good fishing-ground; from the Gordon Arms and the Cottage between the lakes, the angler commands the Yarrow, and the lakes of St. Mary's, and the Loch of the Lows. To fish Loch Skene, it is best to sleep at the Birchen Hill, but it may be reached from the Beatock, from Moffat, and from the Gordon Arms. Kelso is an excellent station from which the angler may fish the Eden, the Teviot, and the. Tweed, but to fish with success the Kale, College and Beaumont waters, he should take his station at Town Yetholm, and at a village on the Kale. The Glen may be fished from Wooler and the Till at several points on the road to Corhill.

CHAPTER I

EDDLESTONE WATER—THE LYNE

The Eddlestone, which runs from the north, and joins the Tweed near Peebles, is a good angling stream, when taken in the right mood. The village of Eddlestone is the best starting point, either towards the source of the river or towards the Tweed. During heavy rains or floods, like all streams joining a larger one, the fish from this latter rush up the smaller stream, and may be taken in any numbers. At those times, when the waters are dark and beginning to fall, little skill is required. A red hackle, with or without wings, is the taking bait, or a minnow fresh or even salted. I have no experience of the artificial minnow, but could imagine readily that it may often answer.

In the Eddlestone are to be found the common trout of both kinds, the parr, the smolt or fry, in April and May, and no doubt towards the close of the year, salmon and sea trout.

The Eddlestone will conduct the angler to the Tweed, near Peebles, and there he will probably rest for the evening. A short walk up the Tweed will repay the toil, if toil it can be called. The Nidpath Castle in ruins is here; an old holding of the ancient baronial robbers. There is also good angling here: opposite the castle I caught my first trout, whilst carelessly sauntering along and trailing after me the line in the river. The fly was a red hackle, which tempted a noble trout nearly two pounds in weight.

From this spot the angler may proceed upwards to fish the Lyne, a good angling stream, which joins the Tweed several miles higher up: but this stream is more conveniently fished from Noble House, and from a village situated close to the river itself. It is called Romano Bridge, and should he find the waters in good order, 1 know of few better streams.

THE LYNE.

The river Lyne runs through a lonely and somewhat narrow valley, shut in by lofty hills clothed with verdure. The country is in fact a great sheep walk. It contains both kinds of trout common to the rivers of Scotland, that is, the common red-spotted trout, and the trout which, having parr markings even in the adult state, I shall call the parr-trout. But besides these, the true parr is found in abundance; and, in their due season, salmon and sea trout, and the smolts of both, fall to the lot of the experienced and determined angler.

In a small stream, which, like a mill race, joins the Lyne a mile or two below the bridge, the pink-coloured, red-spotted trout is said to be found. I fished it, but the day was not favourable. I do not, however, doubt the fact.

Whilst fishing the Lyne, near the bridge, some years ago, I saw approaching me a singular figure, in the human shape, however; he had on a seaman's cap lined with fur, and wore a long blue coat of coarse duffle, girded with a black leather belt supporting a fishing basket; his hand were a rod and tackle. I could see at a glance that he was an experienced real angler. Resolving to speak to him, I stood still as he approached, and was saluted in a very friendly way by name. Known to all the world, I took it for granted that he was someone who had met me somewhere: not so; he turned out to be an ancient schoolfellow. I learned his history in the village; he was a hermit and a miser, and resided in a very small thatched mud-built cottage on the banks of the river. He fished daily, and had done so for many years; Sundays excepted, I presume. He never changed his attire. To me he appeared sane enough: in his day he had been a naval surgeon, a class of men very much to be pitied. If not insane, he must have been of the stoic class of philosophers who hold themselves entitled to terminate existence so soon as it becomes insupportable to them; for he committed the rash act a few years afterwards, as I was told. Alas for man! Why did he live a recluse? And if so, had he nothing to go back upon? No resources within his own mind? Or was it the east winds, that for eight months of the year creep up the lone valley of the Lyne and embitter human life? I have heard the nine of diamonds called the Curse of Scotland; but I rather think it must be the east wind. You may include the east wind of merry England.

CHAPTER II

THE TWEED FROM PEBBLES TO INVERLEITHEN

I have never fished the Tweed from Peebles to Inverleithen; nevertheless, the angler may find excellent sport here. Trout take fast when the waters are dark and thick, or red and muddy. On such occasions, the preserved salmon-roe is a telling bait for all sorts of trout. Tweed trout, it is true, are but sorry fare, but the angler does not heed this. At Inverleithen is the small stream of the Leithen, almost dried up when I saw it. Yet in winter, 1 have been told, large bull trout and sea trout ascend the river to spawn. They are slaughtered, of course, by the country people.

At Inverleithen, Hogg, the so-called Ettrick Shepherd, passed much of his time. Not that he lived there; his house and farm were on Yarrow's braes; but Inverleithen was his favourite haunt, his chief delight being to carouse and indulge in deep potations with strangers and friends. I well remember an esteemed friend who boasted that, with the aid of another, a drunken Edinburgh writer, he had settled the Ettrick Shepherd, who drank so much and so long at one carousing bout, that he was never more seen to raise his head! Hogg was a poet of no mean order; imaginative and gifted by nature. He lived by Yarrow; Yarrow, called classic before his time. I remember inviting him to supper with half a dozen others of the "Homer Craft." As the champagne flew to their heads, they seemed to become almost deranged. They are now either dead or mad in reality. This was not long before his death. A vile crew of scribblers and assassins of character were in the habit of using poor Hogg's name to give a sort of respectability or zest to their malicious monthly filth. They proved his ruin.

Hogg experimented on the parr and wrote about sheep, for he was a sheep farmer, and might have done well under a most indulgent landlord (Buccleugh); but, like others of his craft, he was scarcely ever at home. Here is a picture of the crew by one of themselves; let it be remembered, also, that he lived in a country where whisky is, or was, the universal drink, and of which the immortal bard says:

> "Thou art the life of public haunts;
>   But thee, what were our fairs and rants? E'en
> godly meetings of the saints,
>   By thee inspired,
>   When gaping they besiege the tents, Are
>   doubly fired."

The rhyming crew have been painted by one of themselves, by one who knew the human heart.

> "O mandate glorious and divine,
>   The ragged followers of the nine,
>   Poor thoughtless devils. "

At Inverleithen the angler, who is fond of bold and mountain scenery, may cross the wild and desolate Minch Moor to Selkirk, and from thence fish the lower waters of the Yarrow and Ettrick; or, keeping to the right and southerly, find his way to the Gordon Arms, and from thence fish Yarrow, the Loch of the Lows, St. Mary's Loch, Loch Skene, or wandering by Tweedside make for Clovenford. He will here find in the Tweed some excellent salmon streams, and large trout are to be caught with minnow; but the river is broad and the salmon rod must be used. A deadly bait for the kelts or foul fish running for the sea in May is a lob worm, threaded on the hook and line, so far as merely to leave the point of the hook free; to this attach, by the middle, one or two small worms, and with a rather heavy lead, sink the bait to the bottom of the stream.

From Clovenford to Galashiels is a considerable distance; the banks of the Tweed are tame; Abbotsford, it is true, lies on the opposite bank, and this merits a passing look. It will some day be called "Scott's folly" it ruined poor Sir Walter. But of this more anon.

Opposite to Inverleithen is Traquair and the Bush aboon Traquair. As I looked for "the Bush," I saw a strange looking figure ploughing in the fields, he wore a queue, with powdered hair, and sky-blue swallow-tailed coat, I said to my companion, that man is a Frenchman and a Celt, and wears the costume of Louis Quatorze; he is a Celt, he never alters essentially, and hating labour he never dresses like a labouring man. But still the problem to be solved was, how he came here? So I got off the road, and asked a cottager to whom the grounds belonged; to Lord Traquair, replied the honest Scotchwoman. That is enough, I knew all the rest. So musing on the history of the races of men, I prepared to climb Minch Moor.

And so I did four times; but I must reserve the history of this for another chapter, and so descending the Tweed by Abbotsford, I shall next conduct the angler to the Gala.

At one time the waters about Inverleithen were infested by a few furious drunken cat-o'-mountain roysterers, of whom old Rantipole was the star. The real angler naturally avoids such persons and their haunts. There is surely a medium between such and the mawkish claret-sipping author of the "Salmonia," who never said a clever thing in his life. He was a man of genius, notwithstanding all that has been said against him by the London Doctor who "attempted his life."

CHAPTER III

GALA WATER

"There's braw braw lads on Yarrow braes,
That wander through the blooming heather;
But Yarrow braes, nor Ettrick snaws,
Can match the lads of Gala Water."

BURNS.

A MOUNTAINOUS country, wild, desolate, barren, extending from St. App's Head on the east to the Western Ocean, with little or no interruption, separate the valleys of the Forth and Clyde from those in which run the Tweed, Annan, and Nith. It is in this range of hilly country that we find the sources of most of the trouting rivers of south Scotland, including the streams of the Gala I am now to describe; but on my first visit to the Gala, I reached it from the south. Since then I have fished it at most points. It is a classic river; Burns has made its name immortal. Deeply engraven on memory's tablet is my first visit to Gala, and my last. It was autumn; the autumnal floods had set in. As we crossed Minch Moor from Peebles, intending to sleep at Selkirk, the rain fell in torrents. On the summit of that terrible moor we were enveloped in a thunder cloud. At three of the day it was as dark as midnight; yet we journeyed on by Yarrow, swollen into a fierce discoloured torrent, until Selkirk rose to view. Here we rested; but next morning it brightened up; I almost think it was Sunday morning. Wandering on by Tweedside, we crossed the silvery stream by the bridge, which the traveller will still find a mile or two below the junction of the Gala and Tweed. Thence retracing our steps, we reached the village or hamlet of Galashiels. That we were on foot I need scarcely say. Your anglers who mount on horses and ride to the Gala in post-chaises or by rail are artificial things, called citizens—inhabitants of cities. They are usually bad anglers in the direct ratio of the value of their angling gear. I have tested it over and over again. Someone told me they once met Charles Bell—Sir Charles as he was afterwards nicknamed—fishing in this very water, the Gala. He had come in a post-chaise to Noble House, and when seen by my friend, resembled nothing on earth beneath, nor in heaven above. He was clothed in waterproof, from the crown of his head to the sole of his foot. Had he been made of sugar, which no one ever thought him to be, he could not more have dreaded the touch of water. Poor Sir Charles! he was no angler, but, by the lone river side and on the heaths of his native land, he hoped to escape, if only for a day, the beaten path, the common high road, moral and physical, to shake off for an hour the harness of social life.

The village of Galashiels, when I first saw it, consisted of a church and manse, a sort of inn, or rather public-house, and of some half-a-dozen thatched houses or huts. No one was moving about; it seemed deserted and crumbling into ruins. A coarsely made salmon fishing-rod or two placed over the doorway of one of these low, thatched cottages, told us that there lived a brother angler. We were right. Our fishing-rods and basket bespoke our purpose, and told the simple, honest-hearted inmate who we were. I could not well make out what business he exercised; but of this 1 am sure, he was a noble angler—angler of a higher order, for he chiefly aimed at the salmon. We were at home at once. I distinctly recollect that he was bachelor; but, be this as it may, it was resolved that, for eight days at least, we should fish the Gala. Tweed also was at hand, and a short walk enabled us to reach its banks at that part and near that house which another of Scotland's great minds has immortalized. But at the time I now speak of Sir Walter Scott had not written "Waverley," nor the "Monastery," nor even the "Lady of the Lake" (would that he had never written it!) and the town of Galashiels was a hamlet such as I have described. The lower waters of the Gala, above and below the busy manufacturing town of Galashiels, cannot now afford, I should think, any sport for the angler. It was different then large trout and whitling were caught just below the village. Still, silvery Tweed is not far off, and trout and salmon are no doubt to be taken with the rod. Miles of the Tweed are still free to the angler. Be cautious of its treacherous pools and streams, clear but deep. That fish you see so distinctly, and which you fancy you might almost touch, lies fathoms deep." Still to be successful you must wade. Fish with a small salmon rod, with flies of various sizes; a large trout or grilse fly will tempt a salmon. If the line and rod be not in good order, you may lose the fish, line, and top. It happened that, fishing a little below Clovenford for trout, a seven pound salmon took the grilse fly with which I had hoped merely to entrap a sea trout. He ran the line out instantly; the point of the rod lay in the water for five minutes at a time. I merely held on, and would gladly have been quit for the loss of the line; as it was, I landed him safely at last. But I shall speak of the Tweed hereafter, and so return to the Gala.

No angler need now, I presume, fish the lower waters of the Gala; but he may successfully still cross the highlands by Blackshiels, and crossing from the north, strike the Gala near its source. Here, should the weather be soft and warm, summer dropping clouds appearing ever and anon, a western breeze, and an evening's heavy rain preceding, the angler may still, at any point from near the sources to Torsonse, meet with all success. But to do this he must be first in the field, fish with a short rod, fine line, and red hackle, keep well off the bank, and lose no time. The sun never shone on the Gala while I fished it, for clouds obscure the valleys of the Lammermuir when the Low Countries bask in glorious sunshine. I speak not of Noble House, a favourite resort of anglers in former times. All is altered now, in so far at least as man can alter nature. In the Gala, in my early days, there were salmon and sea trout, parr and parr trout; these still abound. The, Gala was famous for the abundance of parr. But the red-spotted, common river trout also abound, furnishing good sport to the angler, though despised by the gourmand. Like the small rivers which descend from mountains, the upper waters are the best for the angler, the size of the stream and of the fish being often in an inverse ratio. But, whether you fish a large or small stream, see that the tackle be in good order, the reel acting, and the line clear, the footing secure, with space to move a step or two, before you spread your flies, or touch with the minnow (the choicest of all bait) the whirling eddies of the turbulent stream rolling rapidly into the linn, dark, smooth, and deep.

But the art of trolling with minnows for trout I shall reserve for those streams and rivers in which I have angled with minnows. I wish to speak of nothing in which I have not been engaged. I never fished the Gala with minnow.

CHAPTER IV

THE LEADER

To the eastward of the Gala, arising on the southern slopes of the great mountain chain whence the Gala springs: from the summits of the Soutra and Lammar Law, and draining the valleys which stretch from the ridge of this great watershed, southward towards the vale of Berwick, run the Leader and the Whitadder; to these I may add the Blackwater, the lonely Die, and the wild and desolate Fastna. Of these I shall speak in succession, and first of the Leader. The northern slope of these mountains, in its eastern part, supplies the feeders of the Tyne, a stream I have already described. The trout differ. In the Tyne, as we have already seen (Part I., Chap. II.), they are, in many parts, pink-coloured, and excellent to eat; but in the southern waters, of which I now write, they are, with some exceptions, white, soft, and useless as food. Salmon and sea trout frequent both sets of streams, and parr are found wherever salmon are. The contrary of this has been asserted; but I feel certain of the fact that parr are found only in salmon rivers. Is the converse true? I believe it is not. In certain districts of the North Riding of Yorkshire there are streams that are frequented by salmon trout at least, in which no parr have ever been found.

But I return to the Leader. Of this river I know but little; I believe it to be a fair angling water, but not like those of which I shall speak presently. Make for Leader Foot, if you can, from the south: if from the north, march on Soutra, as I did. Let the weather be close and warm, rain abundant, a light breeze to ruffle the surface, and you are sure of some success, at least. Trout take fast during heavy rains, yet on a clear autumnal evening, with the wind at east, I have caught as many trout as I liked in the Boat Pool at Shanna Bank, on the Whitadder. Others, no doubt, have experienced the same caprices in the tastes of trout. But I shall not dwell on the Leader, knowing so little of it. Leader Foot is romantic and most beautiful; the river here joins the Tweed. Beyond, the eye wanders over

Roxburghshire, and the noble Cheviots shut in the scene, but they are indistinct. Dryburgh Abbey is near: it belongs to Tweedside.

CHAPTER V

THE WHITADDER – THE FASTNA

Anglers should have nothing to do with gigs and horses, coaches, rails. I do not even like to mention them. The fishing ground must be reached, no doubt; this I admit. But if you be a true angler, you will turn your back as soon as you can on road and rail, making your way to the sweet valley, the lovely glen, and the hill side.

The streams that feed the Whitadder may be reached at two points. Leave your horse, or horse and gig, should you be unfortunate enough to have one, at Gifford or Danskine, and at once face the Red Brae road of Lammermuir. The misery is that before you return your horse will be starved, and may be injured for life. Better leave no cares behind you, but march at once from Tranent, or Haddington, or Danskine, and rest there for the evening. You pass the ancient town of Gifford, and the sources of the Tyne: Saltoun, also, with its shady woods and rich fields. You are here on historical ground: but go on and rest at Danskine; and when you leave this at early dawn, be sure to take with you refreshments for the day, for you cannot say when or where you may sup.

Journeying onwards from the top of the Red Brae hill, a dark and desolate mountain tract lies before you: no signs of the presence of man to be seen for miles and miles. The lonely innocent sheep bleat and leave you the path to yourself. At last you come to a spot where the road divides. The one to the left, sharp, difficult to find in thick weather, dangerous to take in snow, is the one that leads to the valley of the Whitadder, to Spartleton, and to Millknow, to Cransthaws, and Elmford; it is the one which the angler ought to take. From the point where he leaves the main road, until he reaches Millknow and the base of Spartleton, it is all down hill. He passes Mayshiel, gets a sight of the stream that I have always looked on as the main source of the Whitadder, passes the gipsy's grave, the ruined keep, the junction of the source from the Whitewell of the Whitadder and the Mayshiel stream; and here, a little above the Mill, with beauteous Priestlaw directly opposite, he sits down to rest, and to prepare for the coming sport.

His further proceedings will be regulated by the aspect of the waters. He had better view the stream a little, and look at the Fastna, which joins the Whitadder a little higher up, constituting the third source of this fine stream— unquestionably the best angling stream in Scotland. Should the Fastna be full, running dark and rapidly, swollen by rains which have fallen extensively on its sources, leaving the others untouched—an occurrence I have witnessed more than once— then make at once for the stream, or for any branch that has been flooded. Trout run up such streams in hundreds and thousands, leaving for a time the other unflooded ones, and seemingly the main stream itself.

One lovely autumn day, an hour or so before noon, I chanced to be at Millknow with two other anglers. We agreed to fish different streams: they selected the Fastna. As I had never fished the source arising in the Whitewell, nor angled in the Bothwell —another great source of the Whitadder which joins the stream below St. Agnes—I determined on this course, namely, to ascend the stream of the Whitewell, until I could cross the north-eastern shoulder of Spartleton, and strike the Bothwell, fishing this latter until it joined the Whitadder. Both streams were very low and clear. I saw few trout, and those were large, but out of condition. The walk was too much, for the Bothwell ran winding through lonely glens, making me sad and melancholy, reminding me of some of the streams of Kaffraria— "Het land de Caffren." I do not think I saw a human being throughout a day's ramble of more than twenty miles. My friends who repaired to the Fastna caught six dozen large trout in no time; they were poor anglers, but Fastna, being flooded, the trout ran like mad things up that stream from the Whitadder, leaping at anything and everything.

The glen of the Fastna, looking from Fastna Bridge, is the wildest, and most desolate scene, saving one, I have ever beheld. Woe to the traveller caught here amongst the snows of winter. To sleep amidst the snow is the sleep of death: he awakens no more. Yet the shepherds face those storms, and at night, in search of their scattered flocks. They take nothing with them but a little bread; to taste of ardent spirits is death. The faithful dogs accompany them, and should they lose themselves, they endeavour to regain the banks of one of the streams, which serves them as the thread to guide them through the terrible labyrinth of snow.

As you ascend the Fastna, you will find a bank or scarbrae on the right: it is the identical spot where Sir James Hall first caught the idea that the sandstone strata of the globe are merely sand consolidated under a pressure of ten or twelve atmospheres. In experimenting afterwards on this geological question of great interest, he added a flux of salt to his boiling mixture, and succeeded in obtaining a something like the sandstone elaborated in the chemical laboratory of the earth. He was an ardent follower of Hutton, who discovered the true theory of the earth, the source and origin of all modern discoveries in geology, viewed simply and unconnected with Palaeontology, that wonderful instrument of research invented by an anatomist— "Grand Cuvier," as Byron called him. But Cuvier was greater than even the poet imagined him to be.

The angler may still find the shepherd who conducted my esteemed friends, Messrs. Witham and Allan, and self to the spot; he had also been Sir James Hall's guide through the wilds of Fastna. The geology of the district has its interest, for Mill Know farmhouse is built on a kind of granite, which here comes to the surface. The great mass of the Lammermuir is not however composed of green stone or basalt, but of an older rock, what the Germans call grauwacke, and the shepherds, whinstone.

I must return to trout and angling. The Fastna trout is darker than the Whitadder trout, a circumstance ascribed to the mossy character of its stream: I doubt all this, or if it be so, it is trivial and unimportant.

Mill Know may be reached by other roads than the one I have described. The angler may start from Haddington, and commence his ascent of the Lammermuir at Garvald Church on an autumn day; ride slowly or walk gently. As you begin to climb the hill,' an ancient castle, Munraw, I think, is on your left embosomed in woods; passing onwards, the trees become less and less, fewer and fewer, until they degenerate into mere bushes; the hedgerows dwindle away into scattered patches widely spread, furnishing no fence against sheep or 'horse; still ascending, the grass becomes shorter and shorter, coarser and coarser, more and more wiry; heath appears close to the roadside, and you tread a soil through which the plough was never driven. Look at the vast mountain range before you: it is purple. Soft west winds, as they sweep gently over this field of purple heather, bring with them mellifluous odours surpassing far the new mown hay. The hour is worth an age of common existence. On the slope of the hill, or rather mountain, which closes in the scene on the left, and just as I was about to cross the neck or gorge in which the road lay, a flock of sheep which had crossed the pool beneath were climbing by their narrow walk the mountain side. Some ten or twelve stood still in a row and looked at me. At once rushed upon my mind the passage in the Hebrew record, which I had read when young, but understood not; or possibly imagined to be an Eastern hyperbole; beyond nature, extravagant. But the proof that it was not so was now before me. There they stood in Indian file, as the Hebrew poet described them, comparing them to the teeth of his beloved. "Her teeth were as a flock of sheep newly come from the washing pool." They stood in a line upon their narrow path, level, equidistant, all alike; white, square, like the most beautiful human teeth.

Descend we now the Whitadder, on a warm summer or autumnal day, after floods, a fleecy sky, south-west winds gently blowing, and between Fastna Foot and Cranshaws you may fill many baskets. But you cannot rest here, for there is no place for you to refresh, and your road must be onwards. Descending the river as far as Elmsford, you boldly cross the stream and reach the Cottage, the first of all angling stations in Scotland. At this point you are six miles from Dunse.

THE LONE TROUT, THE SOLE TENANT OF THE POOL - AN EPISODE.

We sometimes hear of the lone star of the east or west, I know not which, at whose dread name tyrants blanch and grind their teeth with rage—monarchs tremble, and courtiers grow sick with apprehension—but of this I speak not. Members of "the order" fish in troubled waters. Whatever is lonely or alone affects us more or less; whether it be a woman or a trout, it commands our sympathies, as the following little story will explain.

It was the end of April, or the very commencement of May, and summer had set in with its usual severity in Scotland, when, mounting my good grey mare, Bess, I at once crossed the Lammermuir in search of quiet, rest, solitude, and health. These I was sure to find on the banks of your crystal streams, gently flowing Whitadder!

The sun appeared for a short time as I made for the stream, for the trout were busy feeding on the early flies, and I soon caught a dish or basket full, but none of any size. But as the day advanced, heavy cold clouds obscured the heavens, the temperature fell, and I resolved to quit the stream which I have never seen since.

About a mile and a half, or it may be two miles, below Mill Know, travelling by the banks of the river, the stream forms a line or pool at the base of a scarbrae. As I approached this, the last time I ever fished the Whitadder, it seemed alive with large trout. They rose at flies almost every instant. At the first cast of the line, I hooked a good-sized trout, and placing it in my basket, threw again. Nothing rose: I stood amazed; for that pool, which an instant before was so full of life and of the finny brood, was now still as death. I mused and pondered. At once it flashed across my mind that I had caught the sole tenant of the pool and stream. To remove it carefully from the basket, to place it gently by the margin of the stream and in water sufficiently deep to cover it, was the work of an instant. At first it lay motionless and turned upwards. I thought it dead. But presently I could perceive signs of returning life. It made a convulsive gasp or two, and springing above the waters, next diving into the pool, it disappeared.

Seated by the banks, I watched for some time to see if it should again appear; it did so, in chase of flies. I felt relieved and rejoiced, as I journeyed homeward, that I had not caught and destroyed the sole tenant of the pool.

Men at a certain period of life lose their taste for angling; but they recover it again. 1 have passed the period, but be that as it may, at no time of my life would I knowingly have taken from the pool its sole live tenant.

ELMSFORD: THE COTTAGE—THE MIDDLE WATERS OF THE WHITADDER.

Of all angling stations in Scotland this is the first, the best. See that your tackle be in good order, especially in autumn, when sea trout and whitlings may be looked for in every deep running stream, or pool, or linn. Approach the river-side cautiously, and rather early than late. Do not be much after ten in the morning. At the Cottage, six miles from Dunse, and at Longformacus you command the Whitadder and the Die. Lower down are some good streams when flooded.

The hills which border the valley, in which the Whitadder runs from Priestlaw, now begin to close in so as to narrow the valley almost to the bed of the river. As if in mockery, one of these mountains has been called Mountjoy; but they are not precipitous nor troublesome to the angler. They are naked, barren, stony, heathery hills, desolate and dreary, but pleasant in summer. The first noble stream you meet below the Cottage is the Greenup, at the first bend the river makes in its course eastward and southward and towards Tweed. If the waters are heavy, and you have reason to think that sea trout and grilse have run up the streams, fish the Greenup with a pair of grilse flies, and a good trout fly above these. Fish it carefully, and failing this, troll the stream with minnow for large trout.

Having done your best, put oh three good trout flies, and fish the river at once as far as the Blackwiel.

To fish this splendid stream and pool, out of which you may take a basket full of large trout and salmon, and sea trout, as the case may be, cross the river above or below the deep pool at the ford. You may find the pool, or drift as we called them in Caffraria, rather deep, so be cautious; I have been obliged sometimes to forego the fishing of the Blackweil on this account, that is, the river was not fordable; but I recommend you to fish it if possible, and this can only be done from the northern and eastern bank.

Of the excellence of this stream I need say nothing, it will never disappoint you. Fish it as you did the Greenup, that is, first very cautiously, with grilse and sea trout flies, next with minnow. If the waters be in good order go on with the minnow. Noble streams and pools await you; the rough water all the way down to Shanna Bank and Abbey St. Bathan's, furnish the finest angling ground in Britain. In the boat hole alone, as it is called, with the water clear, and a strong easterly wind blowing, I have taken, with a pair of flies, six dozen trout. This pool is near Shanna Bank.

Now come the streams and stepping-stones across from the village to the hill-side, and lastly, that terminating in the Milldam. In these streams you may take as many trout as you like. They do not fear the people crossing the stepping-stones.

But should you have time, pass the Mill-dam, and try the stream below at the Whereburn mouth. You may take a two or three pound trout in this stream should the water be in good order. They take fly readily, but minnow is the bait here, and in the next stream below, at the turn where the river is about to enter the woods of the Retreat.

Take care how you attempt to reach Cockburn's Path from St. Agnes, or from the Cottage; dangerous and terrible clefts in the elevated and hilly land intersect your road, in which run the streams that join the ocean near Dunglass. An unhappy man, in the prime of life, returning to the seaside late in the evening, missed his way, and fell into one of these deep clefts.

Happy would it have been for him had he been killed by the fall, for it appeared that, merely breaking the thigh bone, he had crawled down the rocky bed of the stream for many hours, perhaps even days. Rendered furious with hunger, he had, before death, gnawed the flesh off his own shoulder. When suffering from hunger, a sort of insanity seizes some persons. Thirty-eighth hours without food of any kind, and in active exercise during a part of the time, is as much as most men can sustain.

If the angler can find a resting place at St. Bathan's, which I doubt, he ought to remain here; if not, he must either return to the Cottage or push on for Dunse. It is a wild country, without inns or hotels, cabarets, or places of refreshment of any kind. The angler must look to his own resources. He cannot well attempt, when the day is drawing to a close, the road over Cockburnlaw; he must not, in fact, having regard to his personal safety. Return, therefore, to the Cottage, and if the angler be inclined next day to fish the waters from the angle below the mill of St. Bathan's, let him return to this point early next morning, and be prepared for the roughest day's sport he ever saw.

Let your rod be a short salmon rod; your tackle fine but, excellent; your bait minnow; and commence at the bend below the mill of St. Bathan's. Heavy streams follow; there is scarcely standing room to fish the stream and pool; the trout are large and active, and it is difficult to land them. As you descend the gorge, into which the river now plunges, the stream becomes more and more tumultuous, the ground steep, dangerous, and rocky. By climbing the hill, which here rises sharp from the river edge, you lose some streams, but you cannot otherwise descend the river course. I have been assured, that although in floods it is needless to attempt fishing these streams, yet, after long continued droughts, they abound with large trout, which falling down from the Die and the upper waters of the Whitadder, congregate in those deep and dangerous linns. You come at last to the Copper Mine and Hell's Cauldron or Hole, in which they say salmon are to be found at most times of the year; but there is no approaching it with rod or angle.

I had partly fished these wild streams one autumn day, passing many, my object being merely to explore the river banks. At Hell's Cauldron, the river makes a bend or angle to skirt the northern side of lofty Cockburn. I would willingly have explored this, to me unknown portion of the river, from the Cauldron to Preston Mill, where the river, escaping from the mountain gorge, passes into the beautiful vale of Berwickshire, to meander with crystal placid waters by wooded Edrom, Broomhouse, and Allan Bank but the sun was declining, and there remained but about an hour to reach our auberge, wherever that might be. Climbing the high ground to the left, we gained a lonely neck or mountain pass, overlooking the vale of the Whitadder and Tweed; eastward is Blinkbonny, a farm so named,— on which the setting sun fell sweetly,—which I had once some thoughts of making my own, but fate ordered it otherwise. The sun set on its low white wall and thatched roof. Night, with her sombre mantle, began to obscure all things; the labourers had left the fields. Pensive and melancholy, meditating on the past and guessing at the future, we found a resting-place in Dunse.

CHAPTER VI

THE DIE

Whilst at the Cottage of Elmsford, the angler ought to fish the Die. It abounds with large trout; but its lower waters are difficult to fish, the banks being shaded with lofty trees. In a primitive village, called Longformacus, the angler may breakfast, and even find a lodging, should he not be over particular. Starting early from the village, and proceeding up the stream for three or four miles, he will, provided he be diligent, secure an excellent dish of trout before he returns to the Cottage. The village stands in a wild, witch-looking country, dangerous to travel unless by clear daylight. A road, of the loneliest and wildest, leads to Fastna Bridge, another from Longformacus to Greenlaw, by the base of the stormy Dirrington. A footpath through the morass, difficult and dangerous to strangers, usually selected by the natives, cuts off a portion of the main road. If you attempt it, make for some sandy hills of no great elevation, lying straight south, and midway between the road and the mountain. It was at this spot that a villager, returning one evening from Greenlaw, beheld the funeral procession of his sister (who died a year before, and to whom on her death-bed he had refused all means of support) wind along a narrow path, coming, as it were, from Dirrington. He became frantic. As the procession passed him—it was the gloaming phantoms halted, looked, and shook their elfin locks at him. In terror he fled no one knew where; pursued by the fiends which an evil conscience had roused, he seemed to have crossed Dirrington, and descended to the rocky banks of the Die, crossing and recrossing its rapid stream. Faint, wild, and overcome with terror, he reached home early next morning, took to his bed, foretold his approaching end, and calling his son to him, made him solemnly promise that he would never travel by that road.

Years rolled on. The son, strong, muscular, and fearing nothing, yet avoided the road after sundown. But fate ordered that, leaving Greenlaw, and emboldened, no doubt, by friendly greetings and potations deep, he neglected his father's advice, and persisted. He had seen the phantom funeral, and was next day found dead where the footpath is about to enter on the morass on the slope of the sandy knolls, where his father first encountered the spectre.

The seeing phantoms is peculiar to those susceptible of the second sight; but it may extend to millions where the delusion is strong. The delusion of believing that which we see to be always real, the "air-drawn dagger," the spectral funeral, all belong to one class. I met a lady of rank in the Highlands, a Celtic lady, who had twice seen a spectre: no one doubted her. The lady to whom I allude had a brother in Paris, and she resided at the time with, or was on a visit to, a married sister, in the Highlands of Scotland. She belonged to a family of distinction and fortune. Standing, on a Sunday evening, by the drawing-room fire with her sister, awaiting the dinner bell, her brother, who was at that moment in Paris, walked into the room, and after gazing at her for a few seconds, returned as he came. She called her sister's attention to the presence of their brother, but she treated it as a vision, perceiving nothing herself. The matter was talked over at dinner, and thought no more of; but that day next week there came a letter from Paris, sealed with black wax. It was from a friend, and ran thus: "My dear sir, I regret to inform you that last Sunday, about six o'clock, I accompanied your brother-in-law to the Bois de Boulogne on an affair of honour, and I grieve to say your brother was shot dead at the first fire."

CHAPTER VII

THE LOWER WATERS OF WHITADDER

At Preston Mill and Haugh the river escapes from the wild, rocky, mountainous country, entering the beautiful valley in which the Tweed runs. The richest fields succeed the barren waste; woodlands, orchards, and highly-cultivated grounds bespeak wealth and comfort. The river itself partakes of the character of the country, running in gentle streams over a pebbly bed, alternating with long reaches of still water. The angler who would fish these streams successfully should sleep at Dunse, and starting early, in choice angling weather, make for the Whitadder. Preston Mill is about three miles from Dunse, and he may commence there should he think fit, but I have never fished the river from Preston to Broomhouse Paper-mill; from this to the embouchure of the river in Tweed it is otherwise: I know every stream and pool—every rock and scarbrae.

> "The evening's clear:
> Thick flies the skimming swallow;
> The sky is blue, the fields in view, All
> fading green and yellow."

Let us suppose that the angler has decided on commencing below the Mill-dam, and fishing down the stream: that it is August, or the beginning of September, warm, close, and sultry: that heavy rains have swollen the river, making it dark, rapid, and dangerous to cross. Approaching the stream cautiously, and spinning a small minnow, or tempting the finny brood with a couple of large-sized hackle flies, he is likely to hook a large trout or sea trout, or whitling at once. But even without this good luck at starting, by careful fishing, he can scarcely fail to fill his basket with large-sized trout by the time he reaches the bridge and road leading to Chirnside. He will find Chirnside a pleasant resting place: the country between the village and the river is beautifully wooded.

Returning next morning to the bridge just spoken of, the angler enters on a remarkable portion of the river. Without a known cause, excepting it be the rocky nature of the banks, few or no trout are to be seen; they cease as by a miracle near the first slaty scarbrae, where, bending suddenly eastward, the river enters this rocky slaty country; and although it leaves it after a few miles, a short way above Allantown, the river from this to its junction with Tweed has ceased to be that noble trouting-stream which we have seen it is, from the Whitwell to Chirnside Bridge.

Salmon and salmon-trout are occasionally taken in these deep streams and pools of the slaty district, but I never caught any trout there. The angler now reaches Allanton, a village situated at the conflux of the Blackadder and Whitadder. He has his choice of both: but the banks of the Blackadder are, for miles upwards, deeply wooded, enclosed, and preserved, and there is no angling without permission. Salmon never ascend the Blackadder: the cause of this is quite unknown. It is with them, I presume, as with other animals which frequent certain regions in preference to others, guided by an instinct which never errs. In this way Nature limits, no doubt, her extension of animals indifferently. Thus, I question if the salmon could by any means be transplanted to the Blackadder, so as to breed there and annually return. But it would be interesting to test this by placing a few beds of fecundated roe in the streams of this river, near its source; then watching the progress of the fry down the stream, on their way to the ocean. Should they return to their native streams—the streams in which they first saw the light— the Blackadder would then become a salmon river: but this I doubt, for they would not return.

The angler will find in Allanton all he requires; but it is right to caution him, that from this to the mouth of the river I have always found it to be very poor angling. Mills follow mills, dam-heads dam-heads. The river, deeply sunk in its bed, has thickly-wooded banks, that are very beautiful to look at, but greatly embarrass the angler. What the angler might do at particular seasons of the year in these streams, I am not prepared to say. I fished it frequently, and twice at least in the company of first-rate anglers, with fly and minnow, parr-tail and worm, but we caught nothing, or next to nothing. Others may have been more successful; at all events, it is worth a trial. Beautiful scenery will requite the labour of the walk, and by standing opposite a deep scarbrae, where the sandstone strata have been cut partly through by time and floods, I presume the angler may observe a very singular phenomenon. The place I refer to may be about three miles below Allanton, more or less; but I have often observed the phenomenon in other places.

I have said that my companion, on the last occasion I fished these streams, was a most experienced and successful angler, strong and bold in hand, clear-sighted beyond most men. Yet his eyes misled him strangely whilst standing on the bank of the river, and looking intently at the pool before him. In it he saw, or fancied he saw, many salmon, sea trout, and grilses. He threw his' line. They moved and danced about, shifting their ground in a manner so natural, as to deceive his most experienced eye. But I had more experience in this case, for I had seen them before, and knew them to be the reflected angles and edges of the sandstone cliffs, which, rising high above the waters, throw their shadows into the pool beneath. To observe Nature, and to discover the absolute truth, requires, in many cases, more than good eyes and a brain: it requires knowledge or experience, previously-instructed sight, otherwise the object may be before you, and yet remain wholly unseen or unperceived by you. I remember being on a patrol in Caffraria, with a party of fifteen men, commanded by Ensign C— We crossed the great Vische Riviere at De Bruin's post, climbed the high lands running parallel with that stream, and crossing the open country, reached the Koonap River about noon: here I've rested. My friend had never seen wild elephants, nor had any of the party but myself. As we journeyed onwards, I promised him that if his way lay towards the junction of the Koonap and Fish Rivers, a spot I was anxious to see, it being at the time unknown to Europeans, I doubted not our meeting plenty of elephants. It was about three in the afternoon, and soon after crossing the Koonap, we entered on a most beauteous undulating country, with scenery altogether park-like, but superior to any park that ever was modelled by human hands. At the distance of about a mile to the right there ran a ridge of moderately-elevated hills, covered with the bush which clothes most of the hills and banks of the rivers in Southern Africa: a bush terrible to behold— dark, melancholy, and full of painful recollections. On the slopes of these hills, I saw at once a troop of wild elephants of at least a hundred, young and old, peacefully grazing as they travelled along, probably towards the bush of the Great Fish River. I took infinite pains to point them out to my friend C— a quick. sighted, dark-eyed Celt, and to the detachment he commanded, but all in vain: they could not see one.

The detachment being on foot, with the exception of C—— and myself, we left them where we halted, and rode gently towards the elephants, and had come within half a mile, when all at once he saw that what he had supposed to be the naked red clay patches of the hill, intermingled with the bush, was a vast troop of the greatest of all Nature's terrestrial quadrupeds.

Mentioning the circumstance many years afterwards to my most esteemed friend, Dr. Brewster, he assured me that the same thing had happened to himself. An object was placed under the microscope by Sir J. Herschell, and although he did his best to see it, he did not succeed, until Sir John showed him how to look for it.

That incomparable wit, John Barclay, used to illustrate the difficulty of being unable to see what ought to be seen in a different way. To one of his students, who could not see an object placed before him, he remarked – "It is no fault of mine, for as I know it to be there you ought to see it."

But if men are slow sometimes at seeing that which they ought to see, they on other occasions are quick to discern that which has no existence. They may move rapidly without consciousness, believing all the while that they do not move at all; the consciousness of the action is overcome by a stronger consciousness—a belief—strongest of all mental actions—a belief.

THE BLACKADDER

The angler may fish the sources of the Blackadder near Whitburn, or in the middle of its course from Greenlaw to Dunse; either of these stations will be found convenient enough—its lower waters near Allanton, where it joins the - Whitadder.

But its waters are mostly protected, and the stream itself, unless after heavy rains, insignificant. It contains no salmon, nor sea trout, nor parr. Its trout are darker and finer, and rather better eating than the Whitadder trout, which, after all, is not saying much for them. They are chiefly the trout called parr trout, by which I mean common river trout, retaining to the adult condition tolerably well marked parr markings.

The Blackadder would be an excellent trouting stream were it not for poachers, the most destructive of whom are, not the wild daring fellows who break into grounds by day or night and make a dash at what they can get, but the sly wily poacher, who enters some park or grounds, walled and protected, by the side door leading to the home farm or gardener's house, on the strength of a slight acquaintance with the farmer, or the niece, or nephew; a neighbouring Dominie Sampson, for example parish schoolmaster. Once within the grounds he knows where to find a hand or pout net; through the estate runs a pretty deep rivulet communicating with the Blackadder, into which, of course, the largest trout make their way about the beginning of autumn. The fine dish of trout thus caught are quietly sent to the head inn of the neighbouring town. These are the poachers who destroy the trouting streams of Scotland. Not far from the banks of the Blackadder there lived a few years ago a Dr. Hornbook such as the Scottish bard has described! He died a natural death, a circumstance that surprised me. The tragedies that happened in his hands must have been pretty numerous; but he ',vent through them even with credit, and finally came to be employed by the gentry themselves. The public, and especially the wealthy and titled public, prefer, I think, self-taught doctors; the illiterate show a decided preference for the uneducated preacher, and all are agreed that a profound lawyer makes a very bad attorney.

Highly as I value natural gifts, I would still venture to suggest that education may, notwithstanding, be of some small benefit to mankind. Many clever men, men high in office, are of opinion that all beyond reading, writing, and casting up.

CHAPTER VIII

THE TWEED THE TALLA – LOCH SKENE

Some good angling streams join Tweed from the south; the Talla, for example, which indeed forms one of its sources; the Ettrick and Yarrow, the Tiviot, the Till. I shall speak of these pretty nearly in the order I have enumerated. Loch Skene belongs, to be sure, to the waters that join the Solway, and may be reached as well from Moffat on the Annan as from the Gordon Arms on Yarrow. Nevertheless, I shall describe it as I first saw it when, ascending to the sources of the Talla, we boldly climbed the lofty mountain range, whence Tweed, and Clyde, and Annan take their origin.

THE BIELD

The angler will find the Meld or Crook good stations for sport. The Tweed is here, upon which he can always fall back. He is within a short distance of the Talla, and by starting early, he may reach Loch Skene, returning the same evening to the Bield; but he must take refreshments with him, be regardless of fatigue, sure-footed, and speedy of foot. His lungs must be untouched. Linger not on the way. But before I lead the angler to Loch Skene by this route, or any other, let me say a few words about Tweed and Talia.

These streams uniting near the bridge form, as it were, the Tweed. At certain times of the year, and in certain conditions of the river, there must be excellent fishing here. But I never saw the Tweed in good order at Bield, and so had no success. The common trout abounds, and parr are innumerable. They may be taken with an artificial fly during every month of the year. I had this done for me. At no time do they seem to differ; the roe in the female fish being always uniformly small, minute; the milt, on the contrary, in the male parr, being occasionally very large, occasionally very small, but unconnected, as to its growth, seemingly, with any particular season; unlike, in this respect, as in many others, all other fishes.

The Talla will furnish the angler with several days' good sport, and, when swollen with rains, I should think it an excellent stream for minnow-trolling. Large trout must ascend it at those times.

Prepared as I have described, ascend the lone valley of the Talla, and climb the steep mountain which shuts it in at the top. Here the road divides into two; the left leads to Megget-land and Yarrow, the right to the wild country lying between the valley of the Talla and the Gainshope Loch. A footpath will conduct you to the summit of a high neck of land connecting Raven's Crag, at the foot of which is Loch Skene, with the mountain chain which, bending westwards and to the south, slopes to the banks of Annan and Evan Waters.

Keep the Raven Crag on your left, and proceed at once forward, and soon will Loch Skene unfold itself. Dark, dreary, desolate, and mournful is that deep pool of water. Black morasses, precipitous and dangerous rocks, surround it on all sides. The grassy slopes are pitfalls, and lead to the valley of death. It is the wildest scene I ever beheld.

Descending to the Loch, we found in it two kinds or varieties of trout, but none large - nor any parr. As the day rapidly declined, we ascended in an hour or two the hill, by the same route, and making rapidly for the valley of the Talla, reached the Bield extremely fatigued.

Some years afterwards I visited Loch Skene by a different route. On this occasion we travelled from Annandale, ascending the stream which Loch Skene pours into the Annan. It meanders for many miles through a very beautiful but narrow valley, enclosed by lofty mountains. You reach at last a small inn, a kind of auberge, on the highest point of the neck of land, forming the watershed between the sources of the Annan and that of Yarrow. Resting here, we proceeded late in the afternoon of a gloomy day to visit Loch Skene, at the distance of about three miles from the tiny inn. The day became more and more obscured. After fishing the lake, we were foolish enough to propose descending in the course of the stream, which, after a short course, dashes over a perpendicular and terrible precipice, forming the Grey Mare's Tail—a fall of water of great height. To the brink of this fearful bank we approached, on the left side of the stream, descending until the roar of waters, as they boiled in the fearful cauldron below, was but too audible.

To reascend was the difficulty, and even when surmounted, how were we to proceed? It was all but dark. Fortunately, whilst travelling up the valley in the morning by the great road, I remarked that the slope next the gorge by which the stream escaped, though very steep, was a continuous grassy slope, uninterrupted by precipices, as all the others were. By this slope I determined to descend. We escaped with life. Travellers and wanderers have perished at this very spot, by falling into the dreadful cauldron, from which it has been difficult to remove their helpless remains. One such was swept around the cauldron for many days.

Let the angler be cautious how he attempts descending the slopes of these mountains. They are grassy for some hundred feet, when suddenly a precipitous wall of basaltic rock appears, to descend which is impossible. Viewed from a distance, these precipices seem trifling as to elevation or depth, but woe to the traveller who should attempt descending them, or even approach the brink.

We left the Birchin Knoll next morning, musing on the escape of the previous day. Travelling onwards by an easy descent towards the east, the source of the Yarrow accompanying us along the wayside, in a few hours we were fishing the Yarrow at the Gordon Arms.

High up the source of the Tweed and Annan there are streams which, when flooded, find their way partly into Tweed and Annan, and partly into Clyde. It is by these watercourses, as has been supposed, that the smolts, which in some rare instances have been found in the Clyde above the falls, have reached the Clyde. I have no experience in the matter. All I know is, that neither parr, nor smolts, nor salmon, have ever been taken by the most experienced angler above the falls of

Clyde. Their accidental appearance there can only be explained in the way I have mentioned, or by the still easier method of carrying the fish about to spawn above the highest fall.

> "Among these wild mountains
> Shall still be my path;
> Each stream foaming down
> Its own green mountain strath."

CHAPTER IX

THE YARROW—THE ETTRICK—ST. MARY'S LOCH—LOCH
OF THE LOWS

"The hills whence classic Yarrow flows."

The Gordon Arms, and the cottage kept by a lone widow in
a romantic spot between the Loch of the Lows and St. Mary's
Loch, have ever been favourite haunts of anglers, young and
old, honest and false, for they are of both sorts. I had never the
good fortune to fish the Yarrow or the Ettrick when in proper
condition, and can therefore say but little concerning these, no
doubt, excellent streams. The lochs just named contain
numerous trout, and some exceedingly large ones have at
times been taken. Parr also abound, and it was with parr,
caught in Yarrow, that the Ettrick shepherd attempted to prove
the parr to be a young salmon, by cutting off a portion of the
mort fin, or otherwise marking them, and watching their return
from the ocean as grilses and salmon. The farmhouse he
occasionally occupied (for he rambled from home as often as
he could), stands on a rising ground not far from Yarrow's
banks. I never hear his name mentioned now; yet he wrote
some sweet songs, and was no doubt a man of genius. But as
Horatius Flaccus eclipsed all minor poets of his day, obscuring
or even destroying reputations which, but for the great
luminary, would have sparkled and shone, so Burns put out the
lesser lights of his age'. To the south of Yarrow stretches a
vast, naked, hilly country; a sheep walk, in fact, of great
extent. It is Ettrick Forest, but like the Black Forest of
Caledonia, not a tree remains.

Minch Moor separates Yarrow from Tweed. At the foot of
Minch Moor is Philiphaugh and Broad Meadows, and in the
village close at hand, the angler curious in such matters will
find a singular colony of Mulattoes. They originated in one
coloured man, brought, I believe, from India (but not a
Hindoo), who, marrying a white woman, gave rise to this
progeny of Mulattoes. They consist now, or lately did, of
several families. When the gipsies come into the valley, they

talk of these Mulattoes as "our people," claiming a sort of kindred with them; and thus the black blood spreads and spreads singularly enough, under circumstances seemingly adverse to it. Some curious physiological inquiries, resulting from such experiments, will naturally occur to my readers; inquiries which might be and have been extended from trout to man.

Further than what I have said, I have no experience of Yarrow and Ettrick. They seem good streams, but must in many places be sadly fished and poached. Some fish with an instrument called the otter, especially in the lochs; it is very destructive, but I never savvy it used; I have alluded to it in the Introduction of this work.

I had almost forgotten to say that, in the Megget water, which joins the Yarrow, near the Gordon Arms, pink-coloured trout are reported to exist. When I was there the stream was so low as to be Wholly unfishable. It is a mere brawling burn, but not to be despised on that account.

CHAPTER X

THE TEVIOT AND THE KALE

The angler may fish the Teviot at many points, but a few miles above Kelso, from Kalemouth downwards, he will find to be as good as any. It is an admirable trouting stream; in it he will find in abundance the common red spotted trout, the parr trout—parr most plentiful—and, in due season, sea trout and salmon, smolts of both kinds. Early in May, in fine weather, I have seen the pools of the Teviot alive with salmon, descending with the smolts to the ocean. The kelts, or spawn-grown fish, generally refuse all bait. Large fish may be found dead amongst the rocks, seemingly exhausted by their winter residence without food in the fresh water; weakened also by the act of spawning. Those which get to the ocean soon recover their strength and flesh; the insect which attacks their gills in fresh water dies and falls off; and they return again and again to their natal streams.

To fish Teviot you require to wade, and that sometimes deeply. Minnow is your best bait, but the artificial fly answers well enough. Change them frequently, until you hit on the taking fly. Breakfast in Kelso, and, provided with a short salmon-rod, you will reach the Teviot time enough to have a good day's sport. What does the poet say?

> "The huntsman loves the early morn,
> The angler seeks at noon
> The river side and shady bank," &c.

THE KALE

High in a lone vale of the Cheviot, on the path that but lately was nightly trodden by the contrabandists, and in former times by Scotch and English border robbers in search of prey, springs the Kale, a fine fishing stream, but inferior to the Whitadder. To fish this stream advantageously, the angler should take up his residence at a village situated on its banks, about seven miles to the south of Kelso, near the entrance to the valley I have just mentioned. From this village to Kale mouth, where it joins the Teviot, there are many fine streams and pools. Trout of the usual kind abound, and salmon and sea trout ascend the Kale, but I never saw any parr; and 1 have been assured by those who know the river well, that parr are not to be found in the Kale. It is a most remarkable circumstance, were the fact fully proved, but negative evidence is generally defective. Fine walks may be had all around. You are on the edge or shoulder of the Cheviot.

When tired of the Kale, the angler may reach in a short walk the Beaumont and College, feeders of the Glen and the Till. But to fish these without discomfort and extreme fatigue, he had better make Town Yetholm his headquarters for a few days. He is now in Gipsy Land.

Musing on the past, I wander in imagination by the banks of the Kale, and by Tweedside. Where are the friends of my early years? dead, broken, dispersed, gone. Where the rich farmers who rented these farms? depressed, sunk, ruined. The palace, strong and eternal, reposes on its primogeniture and feudal rights: the cotter exists, protected by the contempt which poverty, ignorance, and a hopelessly pitiful state naturally engender. But the middle class man disappears; rent consumes first his profits and next his capital. The little property he had sinks into the jaws of the territorial lion.

It is sufficiently curious that, in the district of which I now speak, the swollen neck, so common in Derbyshire, is met with frequently. This is the land for the Cheviot sheep, turnips, and large farms, and enterprise.

CHAPTER XI

THE TILL AND ITS TRIBUTARIES.
THE BEAUMONT—THE COLLEGE WATER —THE GLEN.

The angler, about to fish these streams, should leave Kelso before breakfast. A walk of about six miles brings him to Town Yetholm. Here he should rest a few hours, arranging his tackle, refreshing himself thoroughly, put on his fishing shoes, and having secured a supply of live minnows, or which have just lived, let him proceed to fish the Beaumont. My first impressions were unfavourable to the Beaumont. I had no minnows, and the water was low. The trout seemed scarce, and the few taken were small. But a short way down the stream, I overtook an aged fox-hunter, a stalwart man of sixty at least, upright, strong and massive, gentlemanly and frank. We met as brother anglers and freemasons do, and were acquainted at once. His tackle consisted of a strong short rod, and good firm line, which he kept also short. A boy attended him with an old tin narrow-necked oil jar; this held the minnows, alive and ready for use; they could not possibly escape out of the narrownecked jar. He fished only with minnow; knew where all the large trout lay; caught them only; and was cool, collected, and pleasant, as became an old English squire of the Vernon breed.

I learned his history by merely remarking that there were good fishing streams in Northumberland, from which I presume he came. "But in fact," said he, "I live here with my family to economise" (he was still, I should think, some seventeen stone weight). "I have a house near the village here, and amuse myself in this way. But in following the Northumberland hounds," I said, you must have known my excellent friend, Henry W— "What?" he said, "Henry W— your friend? then we also are friends, for a nobler heart never lived." And so it was. They had lived like brothers and followed the fox-hounds so long as they could follow them. But a hundred thousand pounds are soon got through in this way. My friend Henry W— economised in the northern capital, and took to mineralogy and geology. The fine old fellow I was then conversing with, having no taste for books or science, rusticated and fished, and well he fished, especially with minnow. To succeed with minnow as a bait, a man ought to be at least five feet ten inches; strong armed, strong wristed. A shorter man is unable to cause the minnow to touch the water as gently as a fly, which it ought to do; but unless he does so, he will always be an inferior minnow fisher. *Non omnia omnibus* is the law of Oxford, although the dons have not acted up to the spirit of the proposition, and a very good law it is. Paley would have said it was so intended, and so no doubt it was, otherwise it would not have been so. But when he pushes this a little further, and argues that it must be a providential arrangement, that all men are not pushing, active, striving, energetic, industrious, he uses a double-edged knife, dangerous to him who employs it.

We left our pleasant brother of the angle and his little rustic tiny page, promising to call when next we returned to the village, and proceeded down the Beaumont; but finding that we really were not duly prepared to fish its short streams and semi-stagnant pools, we returned, determined to try the College water, another tributary of the Till. The Beaumont we have just left arises on the north aspect of the high or great Cheviot; the College, I rather think, from its eastern flank. The level summit of the high Cheviot is said to be a morass, whence these streams flow.

THE COLLEGE WATER
TOWN YETHOLM—GIPSY LAND.

The morning was dull and misty; it had rained a little, but not sufficient to influence the water. It was the commencement of May, and the gipsy tribe was clustered as it were on the slope of the Cheviot, overhanging Town Yetholm. They were still in their winter quarters. In England, the dark-skinned, black-eyed, Asiatic race, boast of never sleeping under a roof. Not so in Scotland. A considerable body exchange annually, as winter sets in, their summer tents for thatched huts. From these hovels they early in May decamp with the salmon fry, which, collecting in shoals, leave for the vast ocean the waters in which they first appeared; so, at a signal, as it were, and in a day, the gipsy breaks up his encampment; all go with them, old and young; they move like a flock of birds, as if not intending ever to return. A return with them is merely a contingent, not a necessity.

As yet, they roosted in the village through which we passed whilst ascending the first range of the Cheviot, over which we were directed to pass to reach the collateral valley in which runs, shut in between two ridges of the Cheviot, the College water a clear crystal brook, winding for miles through a lonely glen, all but uninhabited, and chiefly tenanted by the Cheviot sheep.

As we passed through the village, 1 was anxious to get a sight of some of its inhabitants. Unlike what we find in a Scottish village, nobody was to be seen; ever watchful, ever suspicious. So, knocking boldly at the door of- one of the huts, I asked my way to the College water. Immediately a young woman appeared; the only really beautiful gipsy I had ever seen: she came out to point out to me the road I sought. On raising up her arm, the short sleeve exposed a good deal of the part above the elbow a circular leprous spot caught my eye, and I looked at my companion. She was instantly sensible that I had discerned the curse of the race, and, blushing deeply, retired into the interior of the hut.

We journeyed onwards towards the College water, which was soon reached, for the distance is not great. We were in hopes of overtaking the salmon fry, which we knew were, like the gipsies, preparing to migrate. But in the College water we. found only small trout of both kinds, and parr abundantly. Just as we had begun to despair of seeing the smolt of the season, we reached a small dam head at the commencement of the Glen—the name the united streams of the Beaumont and College waters receive: in this dam-head, retarded by it, and awaiting the first May flood, swarmed the smolt in thousands.

The fry is far from being timid or delicate in its food like the salmon. It leaps at an artificial fly readily, like the parr, in places where the common trout will not look at it. We caught a few, to be quite sure that they, like the gipsies, were there on such a day, and journeying up the Beaumont to Town Yetholm, soon reached our resting-place for the night.

The desire to discover the unknown, in the interests of science only, without any reference to a practical bearing, is a rare quality of the human mind. Paley would say, again, that this is arranged most providentially, else mankind would become speedily a world of theorists, in which all invented and none applied. Laputa, which Swift left traversing amidst the clouds, would descend upon earth, there to rest and to abide for ever. Soon would the fields cease to be productive. Men would be engaged in endeavouring to secure sunbeams in hermetically-sealed bottles; in extracting sunbeams from cucumbers. The quadrature of the circle would not be forgotten, nor the perpetual motion.

But he need not fear that anything of the sort will ever happen in England or in Holland. The natives are wide awake. At any time, should it be expedient so to do, they will call a "hawk a handsaw," but they never mistake the one for the other, whatever be the set of the wind. When my esteemed friend Henry Witham told me one day that it was a curious fact that about the same time he and another foxhunter had both abandoned the chase of foxes for geological pursuits, for science, I could not help smiling. It is possible, I said, quite possible, but see that yon do not convert an honest foxhunter into a wily pseudo philosopher, affecting to look for, in Siberia and elsewhere, that game which he well knows lives much nearer home.

THE TILL

I never fished the Glen lower than the spot just mentioned; but I am aware that it is a good angling stream. Its banks are quiet, pleasant, and have an English look. The Glen in fact, is chiefly in England or on the borders. We crossed the country and sought the banks of the Till, a rather sluggish, slow running stream, but favourable to the angler. I fished it at a stream below the mill on the road to the Tweed. The usual trout appeared, but I learned that the river is frequented by salmon and sea trout, and pike or jack. I have caught perch in lakes when I was a boy, but have been fortunate enough never to take a jack. Yet pike or jack is very good eating, and did I fish for the table, I should not think of despising him. Gourmands tell me that soup made of small perch, quite fresh, that is, taken a short while before, is the most exquisite and the most nourishing of all soups.

In travelling near the Till we saw, one day, a vast tower "looming in the distance," like Tadmor in the Desert. Yet, somehow, it had not altogether the air of a ruin, so we made for it. It was a gigantic folly, the produce of a mind disturbed by the laws of primogeniture, baronial privileges, feudal rights, entail. It had ruined its unhappy proprietors. What it had already cost, I will not venture to say, but it was without a roof, windows, doors, or furniture of any description. It reminded me of what Vincennes would look like in ruins. The rooks flew in and the rooks flew out, and ever as ten thousand pounds were laid out on it, other ten thousand were wanted to repair the damage of last winter's storms. It was a sad spectacle.

Again I visited the Till, but with another companion. We fished the same stream early in May; the easterly wind blew cold, and the day was cheerless and melancholy. Never remain on the stream side when the east winds are blowing, pinching up fair nature's face, and making all things look hideous. My companion was the type whence the clever author of Pickwick has drawn his Alfred Jingle, Esquire. Type, did I say? But for a slight anachronism, I would have sworn to their identity. Even he could not rouse our spirits; so we spurred homewards, crossing the plains of Northumberland, the wooded glades of Berwickshire, and gaining the northern slope of the Lammermuir soon saw the Crag of Salisbury and Arthur's Seat.

Jingle now sleeps, not with his fathers, but with Franklin, at the bottom of the Frozen Ocean, awaiting the next geological revolution, when a new order of things shall arise, and the men of that day, should there be any, speculate on the position which Jingle may have held in the animated creation. He has with him, I believe, three or four feet cut from off the legs of Chinese women, and preserved in spirits. What future geologists will say of this I cannot imagine.

CHAPTER XII

THE TWEED

The Tweed, so celebrated in song, is of all the rivers of Scotland the best suited for angling, and an angler might pass a pleasant week or fortnight in fishing the Tweed from Tweedsmuir to Norham or even to Whitadder mouth, confining his sport strictly to the stream itself. Many beautiful and many wild scenes would he pass through. There are interruptions, it is true, to the angler's course, but fewer, I believe, than occur on any stream of its magnitude. His best course would be to commence at the Bield, well provided with tackle, but not encumbered; for the true angler, like the soldier, should not only carry all he requires with him, but be able to angle freely, to cross a stream, to perform a long march, climb mountains, and be prepared to sleep under the thatched roof or marble-porched hall, as chance or fortune may direct. As an angler he will be welcome everywhere, at least I have always found it so.

I have described the fishing at the Bield and in Tala; silvery streams and soft reaches, running over a gravelly pebbled bottom, lead on through a land of heather and pasture to Peebles. Although I have not fished over this ground, I am disposed to recommend it to the angler. Should the river be swollen, he ought not to attempt crossing it by wading through fords which he knows not. Foreign travel and the incidents of war make some bold and enable them to do that with ease which a civilian, though a brave man, might shrink from, or by attempting lose his life. I was travelling one summer day from Dunse to Millknow, by Elmsford. On reaching the cottage I found the river to be swollen, much flooded, and impassable otherwise than by swimming. Unhesitatingly I entered the stream on my good grey mare, although I had never swum her across but once before; but knowing well that all horses swim, and so fearing nothing, she boldly struck out in water which might be ten feet deep. The people on the other side called out to me not to attempt it, but I heeded them not. I had swum. the flooded Keiskemma on horseback, crossed the Anatolo mountains, and lived for years on the Fisch River Bosch, and so laughed at the idea of being stopped by the Whitadder.

The Tweed runs through a wild country from Romano Bridge and the Lyne to Peebles. With this track of the river I am not much acquainted. At Peebles, the angler cannot fail of sport, whilst lower down, at Clovenford, he is sure to meet with salmon. It is not worth while fishing the Tweed, especially at this point, with a rod of less than twenty or more feet in length; and if you put on a pair of grilse flies, see that the running-line be clear, presenting no obstacles to the run of the fish. I once hooked a seven-pound salmon in a stream near Clovenford; it ran on some forty feet of line in an instant. I held on as well as I could; deep pools formed by heaps of stones, thrown in to protect the banks, flanked me on either side. I moved round one of these with great difficulty, and reached a gravelly and open bank. The salmon now ran directly across the river, and brought the top end of the rod under the water. I could do no more than hold on. At last he fatigued himself so much that I managed to get him safely landed on the gravelly bank. When the angler reaches Kelso, he will find a different mode of fishing for salmon practised. The river is all taken, but the fisherman will hire a boat to you, and assist you with rod, line, &c.; the charge is moderate. What salmon or sea trout you take, you may have at a reasonable charge. I think nothing of this kind of fishing. Commend me to the river bank, taking every chance. It is the exercise, the exertion, the skill required, which constitutes the pleasure of angling now roaming by some steep mountain side, now through the precipitous rocky gorge, or following the stream as it bursts forth from its hilly barriers, winding through woodlands and fields rich in grain. To follow the stream free and unrestrained is my delight, little booting whether the basket be filled or not; there is always enough to amuse, to interest, to induce me to travel onwards, never tired of the landscape, to me ever new, ever changing.

At Kelso, the angler, if a gourmand, may have salmon cooked

the minute it comes from the river. I do not advise it; it has a peculiar odour and flavour. Life is not altogether extinct when placed in the kettle, and it tells on the fish when cooked. I should not think it quite wholesome. Beef may be eaten when the ox has been just killed, and it will be found quite tender, but it is not wholesome. The stiffening of the muscles, which always sooner or later follows the extinction of life, should be permitted to take place, and to go off, before the flesh is fit for use. Crimping Of fish is supposed to hasten the process, by more speedily exhausting the life which remains in the muscles after the death of the animal.

Leaving Kelso, then, to wander down Tweed, the angler need not be told how to proceed. The river is generally open for the mere trout fisher, or the way may be smoothed by means of a trifle. But it becomes broader and deeper as you proceed by Coldstream and Norham, rendering deep wading more and more necessary, more and more dangerous. The double-handed rod must now be used even for trout, and these trout, as an article of food, are scarcely worth eating.

But the angler does not heed this; his aim is health, solitude, and the contemplation of Nature. From this he draws fresh ideas, pleasing recollections, not the less, perhaps, that a slight melancholy may give to them a tinge of yellow sere, which, spreading all around, reminds him that winter—hideous, aged, wrinkled winter—is about once more to strip the forest of its leaves, the fields of their verdant tinge, the stream of its silvery translucent hue, sparing nothing, blacking the field, the mountain; the forest trees, which erst were beautiful, most beautiful, warm, young, vigorous, have now settled down, withered by Time's relentless hand into emblems of soul-despairing decay and frigid death.

With a sigh and lingering look, the angler quits the river side, repairing once more to the busy haunts of men, to return, let us hope, next year to his favourite pursuits, when the leaves are on the trees, and the lambs in the fields.

And now reader, gentle reader, farewell; for if a true angler, you are sure to be gentle. We may meet on Yarrow, by the

Loch of the Lows, or on Ettrick; it may be on Tweedside or by St. Bathan's, near the mill opposite Wherburn Glen. Should it be so, and you of the right sort, we shall soon be good friends, whatever be your rank in life; for as Scotland's poet has written;

> "The rank is but the guinea's stamp,
> The man's the man for a' that."

SOME REMARKS ON THE PROPAGATION OF THE SALMON BY ARTIFICIAL MEANS

AND ON

THE GROWTH AND METAMORPHOSES OF THE FRY

The propagation of the salmon by what has been called the artificial method may ultimately prove a useful measure, but it seems to me to be attended with considerable difficulties. With adequate protection for the salmon, the smolt, and the ova, no artificial methods can ever be required. The ova are protected by being deposited under the gravel; but it is difficult to suggest a mode of protecting the very young fry. After they have become what we call smolts, man is their chief enemy. Should it be ultimately proved that the young salmon remain a year in the river before they become smolts prepared to descend to the ocean, then, adequately to protect the salmon, it will become necessary to forbid angling in salmon rivers at all times. The sport of angling must cease.

Early in winter, when the salmon ready to spawn have entered the rivers, two are caught, a male and female, and the ova and milt are gently pressed from the spawning fish, and received into a trough, and being mixed together, are covered over to some inches depth with gravel, &c. The utmost care must be taken that a constant stream of fresh water runs through this trough, in order to maintain the vitality of the ova deposited under the gravel, and at least six inches of water must be kept over the gravel.

In due time—that is, in about one hundred and twenty days, more or less, according to a variety of circumstances unnecessary to enumerate—the salmon eggs are incubated or hatched, and ascend through the gravel into the waters above the gravel, from which trough, according to the arrangements provided, they may be transmitted into a wide space, such as a wide trough, or, what will far better serve the purpose, a tank or pool, made in the course of a brook, or small stream. Here they must be fed artificially; and this is the only artificial part of the process of the so-called artificial propagation of the salmon. The food best adapted for them has been found to be beef finely chopped; on this, it has been, I think, shown they may live for a year; at the end of which period they undergo the last metamorphosis natural to them during their sojourn in the fresh waters, prior to their descending to the ocean—that is, they become suddenly covered all over with silvery scales, and are then recognised and admitted by all to be salmon smolts or the young of salmon or of salmon-trout, no fresh-water trout being ever known to undergo this metamorphosis.

But prior to the great change, which may indeed be called the great climacteric in the life of the salmon, when in a few days, it may be a few hours, he is about to exchange the crystal streams of a mountain inland torrent for the dark abysses of the briny ocean, in search of food and a feeding-ground wholly unknown to him, peculiar and as yet undiscovered by man; prior to this grand change in the life of the salmon, he has already undergone, and has still to undergo, many metamorphoses. Losing the long, continuous fins connecting him by the laws of unity with the former world throughout all time, he gradually acquires the fins peculiar to the natural family to which he belongs. When quite young, indeed up to the time he becomes a smolt, the young of all species of the salmonidæ strongly resemble each other— that is, they have the same system of colouration, of fins, of dentition. As they grow to maturity, each of the three great natural families lays aside certain characters, retaining those which are peculiar to it. The system of colouring common to all the salmonidæ when young, consists of—1. Red spots; 2, dark spots; 3, parr markings. Of these, the adult true salmon retains only a few dark spots above the lateral line; the sea trout retains many dark spots; the lake trout also retains the dark spots; the river trout retains the red spots. One species of river trout retains the red spots and the parr markings.

As regards the dentition, the true salmon retains of the vomerine teeth only the transverse ones; the sea trout retains, besides these, a single short row of vomerine teeth behind the transverse; in the fresh-water trout of all sorts this mesial row is always double. In the young of all, the dentition is the same.

The great difficulty in the history of the salmon-fry is to determine the length of time it remains in the river from the time it leaves the gravel, about an inch in length, to the moment when it is about to leave the river for the ocean. This period is limited by some to three weeks or a month; by others, it is extended to two years. Upon the correct determination of this period rests the solution of the two important questions, namely, the propagation and protection of the salmon.

THE END

Printed in Great Britain
by Amazon